THE LUCKY COUNTRY

Is the Australian Fairy Tale Coming to an End?

Reflections and Reminiscences of a Long-Term Immigrant

Christo Moskovsky

Connor Court Publishing

Published in 2022 by Connor Court Publishing Pty Ltd

Copyright © Christo Moskovsky

All rights reserved. No part of this book may be reproduced or transmitted in any form or by any means, electronic or mechanical, including photo copying, recording or by any information storage and retrieval system, without prior permission in writing from the publisher.

Connor Court Publishing Pty Ltd
PO Box 7257
Redland Bay QLD 4165
sales@connorcourt.com
www.connorcourt.com
Phone 0497-900-685

Printed in Australia

ISBN: 9781922449955

Front cover picture: English: Black and white photographic print showing a kangaroo painted on the side of a carriage, with two men (on either side) pointing to it. `Australia' is written in block letters above the picture. An inscription on the reverse reads: `painted picture of / kangaroo on our / train in Ludwigsburg / November 1948 / Alex Nypl / (Newman)'. Alex Nypl was a Czechoslovakian migrant who arrived in Melbourne on PROTEA, 23 December 1948. Object no. ANMS0287[052] ANMM Collection Gift from Alex Newman. Used through wikipedia commons.

Contents

Prologue:	Has Australia Lost Its Way?	5
1	Life before Australia	13
2	Australia: Early Days (and Beyond)	31
	Interlude 1: On Nationhood, Ethnicity, Race(ism), (White) Privilege... *55*	
3	The Quiet Australians	69
	Interlude 2: On Communism, Socialism, Capitalism, Liberal democracy... *82*	
4	The Loud Australians	91
5	The Indigenous Australians	125
	Interlude 3: On Freedom *139*	
6	The Media	153
Epilogue:	Is This the End of the Fairy Tale?	163

Prologue

Has Australia Lost Its Way?

Australia, the Lucky Country, is by any measure one of the most prosperous and successful countries in the world. Luck has probably been a part of this success, as has, occasionally, been good leadership. But Australia's unparalleled prosperity has almost entirely been due to the hard work of its people. The Australian economic miracle became the envy of the world. Our continuous (until recently) almost 30 years of sustained recession-free economic growth defied economic science (to the extent that there is one). There are already two generations of Australians who were either too young to remember the last (pre-COVID) recession or were born after it. I first arrived to Australia in 1992 and only caught the tail end of the recession. It has been full throttle ahead since then – well, until recently.

We are emerging from a severe pandemic-induced recession whose consequences will be felt for many years. If nothing else, several generations of Australians will carry the burden of the crippling debt incurred as a major part of the Government's response to the pandemic. But regardless of how highly (or otherwise) we judge our political leadership's management of this crisis, no one would deny this pandemic did not emerge here – it came from without, it has been a disaster which was inflicted on us. But a careful and honest examination of the past decade or so will show us that even before the pandemic had hit us things had started to turn sideways – both socially and economically. There are credible views suggesting that for several years already Australia had been in something akin to a mild recession – only disguised through the sugar hits of extremely high immigrant intakes. Adverse external economic and geo-political forces have probably contributed to this downturn trend. But most of it has been self-inflicted.

It seems that many Australians had become so prosperous and so comfortable, that they became complacent. The serious problems that remain a reality for 99% (or more) of people around world have almost completely vanished here, and many Australians – especially the political and media elites – seem to have lost a proper sense of real values, of things that really matter, and have embraced frivolous and often purely symbolic causes for no other reason than to feel good about themselves.

There are also large sections of the Australian community – mostly ethnic Anglo-Australians – who have developed a deeply irrational sense of guilt. They seem to have succumbed to a decades-long propaganda promulgated by a relatively small number of very vocal activists (mostly from the extreme political left) pushing the view that Australia's prosperity has been built on the back of social and racial injustice and oppression. The fact that even the least well-off people in Australia are immensely better-off than 99% of the rest of the world has stubbornly managed to remain outside of the public consciousness. It is so easy to take the things we have for granted.

There is also a not insignificant section of the Australian community who are too shy or too intimidated to venture an alternative view, to defend the remarkable achievement of an extraordinarily egalitarian nation which has warmly embraced people representing every known race or ethnicity on earth. Many

Prologue

first-generation immigrants (such as myself) are among them.

Somewhat paradoxically, this situation has left us – the new Australians, the many immigrants from all over the world – to speak up for the true greatness of Australia. Having the background of our earlier pre-Australia lives gives us a perspective that many of the ethnic Australians lack. It gives us a sense of reality, the ability to truly appreciate the Australian miracle. We do not take for granted the freedoms, the rights, the opportunities, the unparalleled prosperity that Australia offers. We, the new Australians, can clearly see through the lies of the leftist propaganda.

First-generation immigrants (like myself) can never completely shed the perspective of an outsider – even after decades of residence here. It is widely recognised that first generation immigrants never completely assume the host community identity. Even after more than a quarter of a century here I have not become 100% Australian. It is also well established that long residence in a new country inevitably entails a partial erosion of the original identity. The reality is that I am no longer 100% Bulgarian, either. This isn't something that I am unaware of. During regular visits to the old country over the years I have noticed a growing number of aspects of the local culture that I no longer fully identify with.

In other words, immigration unavoidably involves gaining some new identity and losing some of the original identity. The way different people experience this process of identity (de)construction can vary a lot. With some it manifests itself as a form of identity conflict which can be quite tormenting and hard to overcome. It could well be a major factor why, in an attempt to resolve this conflict, many long-term immigrants choose to return in later life (most commonly upon retirement) to their old country. With others this process is less traumatic. People recognise and gradually accept the reality of a mixed identity and can comfortably live with it. Luckily, I am of the latter category.

As a matter of fact, I believe that this mixed outsider/insider status puts me in a unique position as an observer of life in Australia. As I detail in the next chapter, prior to initially arriving here, my knowledge of Australia was mostly limited to what I learnt from a one-paragraph entry in the Bulgarian National Library's largest encyclopaedia. In other words, prior to commencing my Australian adventure I knew virtually nothing about Australia. This meant that I came with an entirely open mind, completely unencumbered by emotion or prejudice.

I also believe I have the right prerequisites to do a decent job as an observer. I have a keen interest in politics and public affairs. I tend to read and listen a lot more than I tend to speak. I am intellectually curious. I have a reflective and analytical mind (no surprise – I am a professional academic).

But then one could say, you are here because of the good will of the Australian people. You are our guest. You have been granted the enormous privilege of life in one of the most affluent countries in the world. What gives you the moral right to pass critical commentary (let alone, judgement) on Australia and its people? My dear friend Moira Boettcher did not seem to think I was entitled to do that when in 1999, not long before the referendum, I expressed the (heretical) view that it was high time for Australia to grow up and cut the umbilical cord from the British Monarchy. *But you don't understand!*, she told me and I still clearly remember the deeply reproachful look in her eyes.

Out of love and respect for Moira I did not push this matter further, although I will confess I was not particularly impressed with her attitude. I thought – how can you let us in, but then deny us the right to have a different view? But I was also prepared to give Moira the benefit of the doubt. Perhaps she was right, perhaps I didn't fully understand the issue at hand. Perhaps by that point in time (barely seven years after my arrival) I hadn't resided in Australia long enough to fully understand.

Be that as it may, at the time I am writing this, I have been living here permanently for close to 30 years – certainly enough time to come to know the place reasonably well. I also think that I have earned the right to provide commentary on all matters Australian. I believe I have fully honoured the oath of allegiance I made at my citizenship ceremony in 2000. I have always recognised that as an immigrant it falls on me to understand the host community's social, cultural and legal norms and to accept them. I have made every effort to integrate and even assimilate. The worst crime I have committed has been to break a speed limit or two (or six), and I have always dutifully and unbegrudgingly paid the penalty fees. I have been gainfully employed for a quarter of a century and have dutifully and unbegrudgingly donated 40% of my wages to the Federal Government. I have raised two awesome intelligent hard-working girls who are 100% Australian and who are a tremendous asset to their community. They are unquestionably my life's greatest achievement.

And of course I have worked very hard all of my life. You see, I have always been immeasurably grateful to this country for giving me and my family an opportunity for a better life. Working as hard as I can, as unsparingly as humanly possible, has been my way of giving back, of honouring this opportunity. The following episode, I think, is quite revealing in relation to the attitude I took to my job at the University of Newcastle. In September 2006 I was due to have my first hip replacement surgery. I scheduled the operation for the week just before the spring break. Barely three weeks after the surgery I was back on campus delivering my classes. I vividly remember the first post-op class. I was standing in front of my students with the support of a walking stick, struggling not to faint from the excruciating pain. It never even occurred to me to take sick leave. How could I do that? My teaching was my responsibility. To take sick leave was to abdicate this responsibility. It was an unthinkable thing to do, almost amounting to a betrayal of my institution.

I remember a meeting I had one day in the mid 2000s with my then Head of School Professor Hugh Craig – one of the kindest and most considerate superiors that I have had in my professional career. It was one of those regular meetings that the School leadership held with academic staff to discuss performance and to map avenues for further professional development. *It has come to my attention,* Hugh then told me in a rather stern voice, *that your workload has been rather excessive recently.* He was referring to the fact that the year before I had amassed 680 workload points, while in the current year I was on track to go as high as 750, i.e., 50% more than the required 500. *We all admire your work ethic*, Hugh told me, *but you have to slow down a bit, mate. No one can sustain this type of workload.*

I wish I'd listened to Hugh's wise advice, but I didn't. The following year I was due to have a six-month sabbatical, in other words I was going to be away for half of the year. I somehow managed to do the whole annual workload in six months! I typically spent between 60 and 70 hours a week in my office, quite often including weekends. Not surprisingly, it was overwhelming and it was not too long before the utterly predictable consequences unfolded. One night I woke up in the middle of the night with the rather uncomfortable sensation of my heart assiduously turning and tossing around, in an apparent attempt to break out of my chest. When by the early morning this had not subsided, I reluctantly came to the conclusion that

Prologue

I'd better go and seek medical assistance. Praise the Lord for the emergency staff at Mater Hospital. About half a minute after I had described my symptoms to the nurse at reception, I was in and given the royal treatment. The medical staff there were **awesome**. Highly professional, stunningly expeditious and at the same time exceptionally gentle and empathetic. They ran a million tests, they stuck needles in me, they poked me, they scanned me, they X-rayed me and, thankfully, found no serious issues, but I got the message. It was not a message that I could afford to ignore. After that I did slow down – not a lot, mind you, but I did slow down.

In summary, I have been a productive law-abiding member of the Australian community for over a quarter of a century already. The undeniable contribution I have made to my professional field and to the Australian community more broadly has earned me the right to express a view on what is going on in this country. I hasten to reassure the reader that whatever I have to say comes from an entirely positive place, from the position of one who remains deeply appreciative of the opportunity for a life in Australia and who has come to love the country very much indeed.

What feels like a lifetime ago I went to meet my dear friend Barry Boettcher for the first time. He was in his office in the Biological Sciences Building talking on the phone, and I overheard him saying to the person on the other side of the line: *Thank God we are in Australia*. Having only arrived a few days earlier I didn't quite understand what to make of this statement. But it didn't take me long to start understanding and subsequently barely a day passed when I did not say to myself – thank God we are in Australia.

What do I bring to the table as an observer/commentator? Like most normal people I think my life philosophy is a mixture of progressive, liberal and conservative values. I am pro-(sensible) choice and even more so pro voluntary euthanasia. I believe individual freedom is the ultimate value – one which underpins everything that is good and successful in Western Civilization. I also firmly believe that people should live within their means and should not spend money that they do not have. In that regard I could be described as a fiscal conservative. I am non-religious, although I recognise the vastly important role that religion can play by way of providing people with a framework of moral and ethical values/norms. If I do have a god of sorts, it is called Reason. The extraordinary ability to reason that we, humans, have somehow managed to acquire is the ultimate gift – one that sets us apart from all other species.

I do not claim to have the most profound insights or the ability to proffer the ultimate wisdom. I do promise to share whatever insights and impressions I have gathered over nearly 30 years of living in this country and to do so faithfully and without holding back.

A brief note about how the rest of this book is organised. The first two chapters are quite personal and mostly autobiographical in nature. Chapter 1 relates my earlier life in Bulgaria, with a focus on the conditions in which I grew up and evolved as an individual. Giving the reader a glimpse into my formative years will hopefully help them better understand the perspective I bring to the table, and will explain many of the views I have presented in this book. Chapter 2 is an account of how my Australian journey commenced. I thought it would be interesting for native Aussies to know what their world looks like to a complete newcomer. The remaining chapters each critically examines a specific socio-cultural and/or political aspect of life in this country. These are interspersed with several "interludes" – each a short essay-like piece presenting a specific aspect of my life philosophy.

Happy reading!

1

Life before Australia

I was born in Sofia, Bulgaria's Capital, in the latter part of the 1950s. For those less familiar with East-European history, geography and politics, Bulgaria is a small Balkan nation nesting between Turkey and Greece on the South, Serbia on the West, the Danube (and Romania) on the North and the Black Sea on the East. Before World War II, Bulgaria was a monarchy with a parliament and a relatively well-functioning pluralistic democratic system. Bulgaria's Tsar Boris was one of the Saxe-Coburg-Gotha dynasty. Given his background, the Tsar's strong affiliation with Germany was not altogether surprising, with the unfortunate consequence of Bulgaria being a German ally in World War II. This alliance was probably more symbolic than real, however. It seems that Tsar Boris was more intent on protecting Bulgaria's national interests than acting on behalf of Hitler's Germany. Bulgaria's military involvement in the War was relatively small-scale. Notably, no Bulgarian troops ever took any part on the Eastern front. Bulgaria can proudly claim to have been one of just two European nations at that time to protect its Jews (Denmark being the other one). This historical fact is not sufficiently widely known and Bulgarians are not given the credit they deserve for saving our Jews. Tsar Boris himself is credited for having stood up to Hitler and for not allowing a single Bulgarian Jew to be deported and sent to Germany's death camps. The Monarch died under mysterious circumstances in 1943. One widely held view (although never conclusively proven, as far as I know) is that Tsar Boris was assassinated (poisoned) on Hitler's orders by German intelligence agents to punish him for refusing to play along with Hitler's "final solution".

In the second half of 1944 when the tide had already turned strongly against the Nazis, the Soviet Union declared war on Bulgaria. Meeting with little resistance, the Red Army overran the country in just a few weeks. What followed was a pattern that we saw in all of the other Eastern and Central European countries which were taken over by the Red Army and which later became part of the Soviet Bloc. All previously existing social, political and administrative structures and institutions were demolished and a local marionette communist government was installed. The months which followed represent perhaps the most brutal and inhumane period of Bulgaria's more modern history. As part of the new communist regime's strategy to establish and entrench itself, armed militia groups were dispatched all over the country whose sole objective was to physically eliminate everyone who was perceived as even a potential threat to the regime. These militias specifically targeted individuals regarded as local community leaders – doctors, lawyers, teachers, priests. People were dragged out of their homes at gun point in the middle of the night and were never seen again. For obvious reasons no official records were kept of any of this and because of that we can never know with complete certainty how many Bulgarians were struck by this mass-murder campaign. Given its scope, however, there is little doubt that hundreds of thousands of typically highly educated Bulgarians – representing the nation's professional and spiritual elite – were brutally disposed of. It was a deliberate attempt to crush the nation's spirit and any resistance it was capable of. Regrettably, it was so ruthless and relentless that it was largely successful in achieving its goals. Bulgaria became the Soviet Union's staunchest satellite.

Some Bulgarians have lamented the fact that for nearly half a century of communist rule there was never a serious attempt to rebel against the regime. We, Bulgarians, are a disgrace, people would say. Why couldn't we have had our own 1956 revolt (with reference to Hungary) or our own Prague Spring (with reference to the Czech uprising of 1968), or our own Solidarity movement (with reference to Poland from the early 1980s on)? Such critics tend to forget that Bulgaria's was probably the most brutal and merciless communist regime in Eastern Europe, or at least on par with the "sister" regimes of Albania and Romania. Even the remotest whiff of insurrection or insubordination was savagely punished: such unfortunate individuals were immediately imprisoned or dispatched to one of the numerous concentration camps that mushroomed all over the country in the years following 1944. Or they just (were) disappeared overnight and were never seen again.

Growing up in the 60s and 70s in communist Bulgaria was no fun. By then food rationing was over, but finding anything apart from the most basic staple foods was next to impossible. To many Aussies, especially those who were born and raised here in Australia, it would sound unimaginable that the humble banana could be one of the greatest and most craved for delicacies; that was exactly the case in communist Bulgaria of the 60s and 70s! Obviously Bulgaria's climate is not well suited for growing bananas locally, but here were Greece and Turkey, right next door, where this more tropical fruit and many others were produced in great abundance. How much would it take to import some, one could reasonably ask. There was, however, nothing reasonable in how the communist government in Bulgaria (and elsewhere) operated. Greece and Turkey were "evil" capitalist nations. Even worse, they were members of NATO. They were "the enemy"! Even the most marginal and superficial trading relationship with them was off limits. Trading with the "sister" nations of the Warsaw Pact was OK. Only they were as poor and as economically destitute as Bulgaria and could offer nothing really worth trading. Once or twice a year the regime would import bananas from communist Cuba. This was invariably timed to coincide with some date or anniversary of symbolic significance to the regime. Their not too subtle message was – see how good and generous we are to you. Let us celebrate this "momentous date"! As a ten-year-old I was too young to appreciate the message, but I did adore the bananas. Having a banana – what a stupendous treat!

There were also noticeable shortages of very basic household items, which continued right until the collapse of communism in Europe in the late 1980s and early 1990s. One of the more serious challenges for the ordinary Bulgarian was supplying the home with toilet paper. I am not kidding. This was one of innumerable articles that the industrial "might" of the communist state never managed to produce in adequate amounts. Toilet paper appeared on the market only sporadically and only randomly – in a supermarket here or there, but never across the whole retail sector. Those who have not experienced first-hand lack of toilet paper probably cannot fully appreciate the essential nature of this product for normal daily functioning. Its incidental occurrence caused these sudden mass migrations across the city as soon as there was a rumour that some of it was available at some shop somewhere. *They have toilet paper in Mladost* (an outer suburb of Sofia), a neighbour would helpfully disclose and there you were on the next bus to Mladost in a crowd of anxious Sofianites desperate to ensure a weekly supply of the precious product. I must give it to the communists – the sense of accomplishment when you eventually managed to get your hands on a few rolls of toilet paper was unparalleled. I certainly do not remember ever experiencing anything remotely as thrilling and satisfying when shopping at Coles or Woolies.

It would take an entire book to comprehensively describe the full range of shortages that we had to put up with as part of our daily lives, including periods of rolling blackouts due to the state's inability to ensure the generation of sufficient electricity. But this is not what this book is about, so I will go no further on this topic. Besides, even though the shortages were a daily nuisance and sometimes a considerable inconvenience, they were by far not the most disagreeable aspect of life under communism. The worst shortage of all was individual freedom. Those more fortunate ones who have never been denied freedom would find it very hard to properly comprehend what being unfree is like. I do not believe many people in the West truly appreciate the enormity of being free. I do not believe many people understand that individual freedom has perhaps been the single most important determinant of the success and prosperity of Western civilization. I will have more to say about this later.

But to return to my point, there is little doubt that the biggest deficit of all in communist Bulgaria (and elsewhere in the communist world) was individual freedom. The country was in essence a giant prison. Notably, its prison-like nature was not solely manifested in people's inability to leave the country at will. There were severe restrictions on practically everything ordinary people could do inside. Someone else decided whether you can reside in the country's capital city or not, whether you should occupy a two- or a three-bedroom apartment and in which suburb, whether you can take up a university degree, whether you will (ever) get a promotion. Admittedly, with the passage of time conditions gradually became more relaxed, especially in the final decade of the regime's existence when people were given a bit more latitude in terms of how much they could manage their own lives. But even then any real or perceived act of political insubordination was brutally punished. Even in the final decade of the regime's existence I knew of people who were thrown in prison solely for telling a political joke.

As I said earlier, growing up in Bulgaria in the 1960s and 70s was no fun. There were four of us in my family: my father Goran, my mother Zdravka, my sister Marta, and myself. My dad was a medical doctor, my mother was a German language teacher. In a different social context, we would have been a very typical middle-class family. In the context of communist Bulgaria, we were pariahs. We were actually pariahs twice. On the one hand we were representatives of the intelligentsia which the communist regime always regarded with mistrust and even hostility. On the other hand we had been branded as "untrustworthies". Not because of anything that my mother or my father had ever said or done to invoke the regime's wrath, but solely by virtue of being a blood relation to people who had "sinned". In communist Bulgaria you paid for the sins of the fathers full time. Before the War my granddad (on my mother's side) had run a small-scale business representing evil Germany's IG Farbenindustrie. After the War his business was dismantled and he was deposed of all of his possessions. And because this was not enough punishment for his "sins", he was never again allowed to work, anything. Well, at least they did not send him to a concentration camp, praise the Lord for small mercies! On my father's side there was an even greater "sinner". One of his much older sisters, Aunt Ivanka, had been working as an English interpreter at the United States Embassy in Sofia. It is unclear whether the repercussions for her would have been as severe if by the end of the War she had terminated her employment there. She unfortunately made the rather grave mistake to continue working at the Embassy after the War. It was a mistake that is not too hard to understand. In these early days people still did not have an adequate idea of the monstrous nature of the new regime. Besides, on the backdrop of the abject poverty that was the norm in the post-war years, as a US Embassy employee she received what could faithfully be described a princely wage. Had she known what was due to happen to her, she would undoubtedly have given up the princely wage, gladly. One fine day in 1950 she literally disappeared off the face of the earth. She had gone as usual to work at the Embassy in the morning, but she never returned home in the evening. A very worried Moskovsky family made numerous inquiries – with the Embassy, with the police, with local hospitals – all in vain. Several months passed before the authorities finally relented and notified my dad that his sister had been detained and deported to the regime's perhaps most infamous concentration camp – on the Island of Belene, off the coast of the Danube. She had been accused of spying for the Americans. Bear in mind that there was no formal inquiry, no evidence, no judicial process of any sort. Aunt Ivanka was simply grabbed from the street and shipped off to Belene.

As unannounced as she had disappeared, three years later Aunt Ivanka turned up at our door step, pale and thin as a rail. I think in subsequent years my parents never ceased to be amazed that she had survived the utterly unimaginable conditions of the Belene camp. My Aunt Ivanka lived for another three decades. I was a frequent visitor to her home. She gave me and my sister English lessons. I never once heard her utter even a word about the camp or anything she had been through there. Speak of the "fear of God"…

Pre-teen adolescents do not yet have the cognitive capacity to understand, let alone conceptualise, the nature of their personal circumstances, particularly when there is no basis for comparison. They accept their reality for what it is and make the best of it. My parents worked unsparingly to provide for my sister and myself, to ensure we have a roof over our heads, that we get a decent meal, that we are properly clothed. Even more importantly, they provided us with plenty of love and care, and because of that we had a reasonably happy childhood. In these early years we, the kids, were still unaware of the stigma attached to our family, but the stigma was there nonetheless. One rather disturbing example from my primary school years would give you a sense of how much the stigma was a part of our lives. It must have been in Year 3 or 4. I had formed a strong friendship with another boy, Yanko. Both of us adored Mark Twain's book *Tom Saywer*. We each had read it at least a hundred times. It was not long before he was Tom and I was Huck, and that was how it remained for the rest of our lives. We were pretty much inseparable, spending almost all of our free time together, often visiting each other's homes. At that time I was unaware that my best buddy was from a rather prominent communist family – both of his parents were some high-ranking party functionaries. But even if I had known it I do not think it would have made any difference to our friendship. Since when do such things matter to a ten year-old? It did matter to others, although I only found out about that a couple of decades later. One day Yanko had been visiting me at my home. He was just out the door of my apartment block when one of our primary school teachers came across the street. *Where have you been*, she asked him. *I was with my friend Christo*, he answered. *You shouldn't be spending your time at their home*, she scolded him, *they are a bourgeois family!*

Imagine saying this to a ten year-old child! Surely she could not have thought that Yanko properly understood the meaning of 'bourgeois'. But in the context of communist Bulgaria 'bourgeois' was a nasty brand, in effect – a verdict. It meant – they are not one of us, they are the enemy! Yanko and I were young adults when he finally shared this story with me. To remember it after all of these years, this incident must have left a profound mark on him.

To give credit where credit is due, it made absolutely no impact on his attitude to me or on our friendship. Although in subsequent years our lives took different paths and we were no longer as frequently together, we did remain faithful friends until he passed away, not yet 50, due to a massive heart failure. May his soul rest in peace!

Ignorance is bliss, as they say. Being ignorant of the stigma certainly made my adolescent life easier and happier. I was academically bright and performed well at school without being too nerdy to stop me from having a reasonably normal social life. Upon finishing secondary school I was able to gain entry into the German Language High School (we called it 'Gymnasium' in the European tradition). It was an elite selective school which provided an essentially immersion type of education. Half of the subjects were taught in German, often by German native speakers coming from East Germany – the so called German Democratic Republic which until Germany's reunification in 1989 remained part of the Soviet Bloc.

I do not think that at that time I truly appreciated the high-quality education I received at the German Language School. Such types of recognition only come later in life, with maturity. By the time I completed the five-year program I was fully fluent in German. I cannot claim much credit for that. For one reason or another, I never warmed up to the German language and my engagement with my German studies was at best reluctant. English had captured my heart and most of my interests focused on things related to the English language and culture. Remember, this was the 1970s – perhaps the most prolific period of the rock and roll era. We were literally crazy about English rock. Because of the "iron curtain", getting access to this music was not easy or straight-forward, but things did filter through – usually on illegally imported tapes, more rarely on records. Many readers probably will not even remember the cassette players, let alone those massive tape decks with their giant tape reels. I do remember them fondly though, because it was on one of them that I first heard *Abbey Road*, *Led Zeppelin II*, Deep Purple's *Machine Head*, Ten Years After and many more.

I was also a voracious reader of English and American literature. I devoured any fiction written in English that I could get my hands on – from sublime immortal classics like Jane Austen and Charles Dickens to the escapist entertainment of the detective fiction of Agatha Christie and Raymond Chandler, and even the much more modest, in literary terms, but still very entertaining James Hadley Chase.

It was my love for English literature that was at the core of my decision to take up a university degree in English language and literature at Sofia University – "English Philology" as the program was called, again in tune with the European tradition. I saw this as an opportunity to read the authors I admired. I also aspired to become a translator and one day translate into Bulgarian some of the works of fiction that I loved so much.

But you know the saying about the best-laid plans. My naïve vision of what my English literature studies would involve turned out to be a complete mirage. As it soon transpired, my ideas about what was worth reading and studying were not particularly well aligned with the English and American literature program at Sofia University. It was not long before I "discovered" that the most esteemed authors of the English language were Thomas Hardy and Theodore Dreiser. As far as I am concerned, it could be very hard to find more humourless and less depressing writers in the English-speaking tradition. If I had been attracted to this type of fiction, I might as well have taken up German Philology and done Goethe and Schiller! And even in those rare cases when we did study an author that I truly admired, like John Steinbeck – which of his novels do you think we were directed to examine? *The Grapes of Wrath*, of course, which is as humourless and as depressing as anything Hardy or Dreiser ever produced. It was as if they had never heard of *East of Eden*, one of the greatest literary masterpieces of all time.

To cut a long story short, my engagement with English and American literature at Sofia University was a bitter disappointment. It was not long before my earlier enthusiasm for literary studies withered to a size which a microscope would struggle to detect, and from then on I rarely set foot in a literary lecture.

Fortunately there was a silver lining. More than a silver lining, actually. More like a true revelation. As part of my program, I was also doing first year morphology. This course was my initiation into linguistics. From week 1 I was thoroughly and irreversibly captured. I soon knew that there was no turning back and that for the rest of my life I would remain, formally or informally, a language enthusiast and a student of linguistics. Looking back 40 odd years on, I gratefully recognise how lucky I have been in discovering this absolutely fascinating field. The study of language has never given me a dull moment in all these years.

The fascinating nature of language aside, I think another factor also played a role in turning me to the "dark side". Everything that we learned at school and university was thoroughly saturated with ideology and communist propaganda. Indeed, in many cases there was little or nothing else! Take my literary classes, for instance. Most of the time it was not the literary works themselves that we talked about. Most of the time we "explored" the "profound" insights which this or that literary critic had offered, invariably from a Marxist standpoint. The linguistics classes were in stark contrast in that regard. They were completely void of any politics and/or ideology, which for communist Bulgaria of the late 1970s and the early 1980s was practically unprecedented. My then linguistics professors deserve great respect not only for their competence and professionalism, but also for their civic courage. People who have not lived in these conditions probably cannot fully appreciate the magnitude of the risk, professionally and personally, that my linguistics professors were taking in offering conceptual content uncontaminated by ideological crap. I will think of them kindly and gratefully until the end of my days.

Adolescence and young adulthood are a period of strong cognitive and psychological growth, a period when personalities are formed and character is built. It is also a period of growing awareness and understanding of the world around us. For me personally the late teens and the early twenties were also a period of a growing realisation of the "joys" of living in a communist dictatorship. Day after day I experienced the reality of what I cannot do, what I cannot say, what I cannot have. It was a period of growing frustration with, and even resentment of, the world in which I was living.

It also was a period of growing appreciation of the undeniable superiority of Western capitalism. The regime's propaganda machine worked relentlessly to promote the "virtues" of socialism and to decry the alleged "evils" of capitalism, but abundant evidence to the contrary was in plain sight. Somewhat ironically, the regime's nomenclature themselves were responsible for providing some of the evidence. There was clearly little doubt in their minds which products were superior, because they invariably chose Western brands over the "triumphs" of the local industrial effort. You never saw them driving a Volga (let alone the humble Moskvitch). They had a weakness for the products of West Germany's automotive industry, with a particular fondness for black Mercedes limousines. So there was the evidence – right in front of our eyes. On the one hand we had the automotive "marvels" of East Germany – the Wartburg and the Trabant, and on the other we had the Volkswagen, the BMW and the Mercedes. Was there a person with an IQ above room temperature who could not appreciate the difference? I don't think so. Indeed, East German cars were openly despised and ridiculed by ordinary Bulgarians. Did you know that the (2-stroke engine) Wartburg was the longest car in the world? Well, yes – three metres of car and 15 metres of smoke behind.

And of course it was not just the cars. Virtually everything that one could think of was produced in higher quality and (much) greater abundance in the West. We literally idolised the West and admired every single aspect of life in it. We obviously admired (and not a little envied) the West's affluence. But even more than that we admired its superiority in science and technology. We were continuously in awe of the West's unparalleled creativity in music, literature, theatre, visual arts, architecture, you name it.

It would probably come as no surprise to my readers that after over a quarter of a century of life in Australia my admiration of Western democracy has subsided somewhat. My views of communism have remained essentially unchanged, though. More about this later.

But communism notwithstanding, life rolled on and followed its natural course. I completed my university degree and started work as an English language teacher at a high school in one of Sofia's poorer suburbs. A year later I was able to get a competitive teaching position at the prestigious Postgraduate Institute for Foreign Languages, which was a substantial career advancement. Meanwhile I married my school sweetheart Violetta and we were blessed with our gorgeous baby daughter Neda, and the equally gorgeous Ellena three years later.

And of course among all of this 1989 happened. How 1989 came to happen and why it happened is a fascinating question which is likely to keep generations of future historians busy. But those of us who witnessed all of this first hand, indeed were active participants in what occurred – we do not really need the historians to tell us the enormity of what started in 1989 and evolved in the years that followed. That was the time when the Soviet empire literally crumbled and after nearly half a century of complete Soviet domination and control a number of East-European nations managed to regain their autonomy and to start the difficult transition from totalitarian rule to a Western-style liberal democracy. It was a time of grand upheaval when existing social, cultural, political and institutional structures were dismantled and were replaced with new ones – with all of the inevitable social disruption that this caused. After decades of social and political hibernation this was a period of frenzied emotions and boundless expectations; a period of infinite interpersonal discussions and stormy public polemic; a period of enormous hope and not a little apprehension. Even more importantly, it was a period of great mental and spiritual transformation, a period of considerable shift in individual and national mentality, a period of freeing of people's minds – a sort of modern-day renaissance.

On a personal level, being a part of this massive social and political change was a truly exhilarating experience, and I consider myself exceptionally lucky to have had the opportunity to be directly involved in it. For the first time in my life I attended a political rally. For the first time in my life I opened up the pages of an opposition newspaper. For the first time I voted in free democratic elections. We were overflowing with optimism and hope. It was happening. We were taking our country back and were building an awesome new future for ourselves.

And then the unimaginable happened – we lost the elections.

Outside of the Capital and some other larger cities, the country had overwhelmingly voted for the old communist party, giving them an absolute majority in parliament. Clearly not everyone was ready for freedom. This outcome nearly crushed our souls. It was then that that we first experienced doubt. It was then that we started to lose our complete certainty that all would be well and that only within a year or two we would (almost) seamlessly turn into a thriving Western democracy.

In the months that followed, our doubts grew deeper and deeper and gradually turned into despair. We could clearly see our country being torn apart and plunged into political and economic abyss by a new political class whose sole objective was to plunder the country's few remaining assets in order to build their own personal fortunes.

Things were going from bad to worse, with country-wide shortages of even the most essential staple foods, like milk and flour and cooking oil. What we were living through at this point (nearly) made us feel nostalgic for our earlier life under communism. During the winter months of 1990/91 it was not uncommon to see in the streets of Sofia large trucks with foreign aid surrounded by crowds of desperate people. These sights made you wonder whether you were in some ravished by war third-world country rather than in the capital of a European nation.

With all of this transpiring it was inevitable that the moment would come when we would ask ourselves the question – can we realistically hope to be able to build, in this country, a reasonable life for ourselves and, more importantly, for our baby girls or should we look elsewhere? If there was a silver lining, it was that now we were free to go wherever we wanted. And we decided that we should go.

As we soon came to realise, "going" was easier said than done. Going was not simply a matter of packing a few bags and catching the next train or plane. It was a wide world out there. Where exactly do we go? And "going" involved more than picking a desirable destination – we needed a visa, and these were not easy to get. Eventually we came up with the idea for me to get admission into a graduate program at a Western university. This would secure the visas, but even more importantly – a doctoral degree would be a good career building move, one which could pave the way to a respectable job in a new country.

But where? It clearly made no sense to go to a country whose language neither of us spoke. As I mentioned before, I had near-native fluency in German, and in retrospect Germany would have been a sensible, practical and relatively easy option. But given my (irrational) distaste of anything German, I was adamant that it had to be an English-speaking country, which in effect limited our options to three: the United Kingdom, North America or Australia. That we eventually chose Australia as our destination was much more driven by emotion than reason. Not that we knew that much about the place, but the "green continent" had such an irresistible appeal – an idyllic remote (albeit sizable!) island in the midst of the Pacific, an ecologically pristine enclave, a true paradise on earth.

Nowadays prospective students applying for admission to an Australian university simply complete an online form, regardless of whether they are located within walking distance of the institution or are on the other side of the world. But how did you do it from halfway around the globe in the pre-internet era? It staggers me to think that there already is a whole generation out there who have never experienced the reality of snail-mail (among other things).

I knew of the existence in the National Library of a massive reference book – something like a comprehensive listing of the world's tertiary institutions. From it I harvested the addresses of two dozen Australian universities and wrote them letters expressing an interest in undertaking a doctoral program in linguistics. It brings a smile to my face when I remember that I hand-typed the letters on my mechanical typewriter. How many of our internet generation have even seen, let alone used, one?

It took a while before we received any responses. Bear in mind that it took between two and three weeks for a letter to travel in one direction! The most welcoming response we got was from the University of Newcastle. They had actually even enclosed the application form that I was required to complete. This settled it – it was going to be Newcastle.

I must disclose (with a shade of embarrassment) that until we initiated the letter campaign I had not even been aware of the fact that there was an Australian Newcastle. It just comes to show you how little we knew about Australia. But do not judge us too harshly – we did not have Google then. Indeed, we had had the opposite of Google – an iron curtain.

In an attempt to find out more about the place I again visited the National Library and borrowed their largest encyclopaedia – volumes and volumes of tiny print. Nearly 30 years later I still clearly remember the entry for Newcastle, New South Wales, Australia. It comprised a short paragraph of no more than a hundred words! Newcastle, located on Australia's East coast, 150 km North of Sydney, was described as the centre of the largest coal-mining operation in the country. I did not then have any issues with coal (still don't), but it was the reference to the local climate that I found much more fascinating. According to the encyclopaedia, the Sydney-Newcastle region had a larger number of sunny days per year than almost anywhere else on earth. The sunniest place in the world? That was a worthy destination!

Over the following 18 months most of our attention was devoted to putting things in place for the planned Australian departure. This phase of the adventure is not worth describing in copious detail, although our preparations undoubtedly generated a considerable amount of postal traffic – between Sofia and the Australian Newcastle, but also between Sofia and Belgrade where the nearest Australian embassy was located. It was around that time that our greatest vulnerability became painfully exposed. Money, or rather the complete lack thereof. Very much like the majority of ordinary Bulgarians, our monthly wages barely managed to keep us afloat and we did not have a single penny in savings. But now our anticipated departure crucially required rather substantial funds – for tuition fees, for airfares, for living expenses, etc. Thank God for a handful of faithful friends who were prepared to dig really deep in order to help us.

Our current situation was additionally complicated (in the nicest possible way) by the arrival of beautiful Ellena at the end of March 1992. Violetta and I very reluctantly came to the realisation that it would be practically impossible for all four of us to leave together. I had to assume the role of the "grand explorer" – go there on my own first and settle in, find a job, create the conditions which would enable my beloved females to join me.

In mid July 1992, equipped with an Australian entry visa and having secured a spot on a transcontinental flight, I was ready to set in motion the grand design that we had been planning for nearly two years.

2

Australia: Early Days (and Beyond)

This first flight to Australia was a rather unforgettable experience in its own right. Prior to that I had only been on a plane once, an internal flight on a Russian made AN-24. Switching from the AN to a Boeing is like switching from a Trabant to a Rolls Royce – from bumpy and noisy to smooth, quiet and luxurious. And the amounts of exquisite meals and expensive alcohol they dished out those days! Nothing like the pitiful portions of bland food you get nowadays.

After around 20 hours in the air we finally started descending towards Melbourne and another memorable moment. Shortly before landing the airhostesses moved along the aisles spraying some stuff into the air. God forbid if we brought in some undesirable bug or virus.

The disinfection aside, Melbourne from high above was a staggering sight, a seemingly infinite sea of residential suburbs stretching all the way to the horizon.

In the wake of our previous stops at Dubai and Singapore, Melbourne airport looked shabby, but remarkably efficient and well organised, and within a couple of hours after landing I was ready to get on my flight to Sydney.

On the backdrop of my life experience with all kinds of uniformed officials, my seamless passage through passport control was another memorable moment. The guy briefly looked at my passport, stamped and handed it back to me wishing me good luck. And an equally seamless passage through Customs. The Officer waved me through, deliberately ignoring the fact that I was bringing in almost twice the allowed amount of cigarettes (dutifully declared on my customs card).

But the anticipation of a cigarette or two after clearing customs was soon quashed. Another shock – all airports and internal flights were smoking-free zones, public transport too. Fines up to $200. Go have a smoke if you think you can afford it.

Then another thankfully much shorter flight to Sydney. The journey on the *City Express*, the bus service that took me from Sydney International to the City Centre (and the train station), was one of my more traumatic early experiences in Australia. Apart from the insane speed with which the bus was moving through some very busy streets, incoming traffic was all on the "wrong" side of the road creating a disconcerting sense of an imminent crash.

At Central I used a payphone (no, we did not have smart phones then) to call Irene Hall – that was the student hostel where the University had allocated a room for me. Sometimes the silliest and most trivial things can impress us, and this payphone certainly did it, including the unusual fact (for me, at least) that a public phone was in working order. Not having a clue what the call would cost, I had inserted a dollar coin just to make sure that I would not be cut off in mid-call. I finished the call all right and when I hung up the phone coughed back 60 cents. Wow! What an impressive technology!

I was a lot less impressed with the train journey to Newcastle. I had already been on the road (metaphorically speaking) for well over 30 hours, but the time it took us to cover the rather modest 150 km between Sydney and Newcastle seemed even longer than that, almost interminable. The train stopped at around two dozen stations and when it moved, it barely surpassed the speed of a crippled turtle. In the nearly 30 years I have already resided in Newcastle, this city has undergone a lot of change – all positive. One thing which has not changed is the railway trip to Sydney, still a 2.5 hour journey, a 19th century "solution" to 21st century public transport.

Another thing that depressed me on the trip to Newcastle was not directly related to the train or the trip itself. Before the train, I had had few opportunities to interact with the local population and little exposure to the local variety of English. On the train I was sitting just in front of two middle-aged females who were making no effort to keep their voices down, and I couldn't help overhearing the conversation between them. Overhearing, however, did not mean understanding. My initiation to the Australian variety of English lasted nearly an hour during which I was barely able to comprehend a word or two. For someone who boasted a tertiary degree in English language and literature and had already worked as an English language teacher for several years, it was a rather underwhelming experience. To think that I had lived under the illusion that I was coming equipped with a reasonable command of English!

But of course at this point I did not realise that mine was not an entirely exceptional experience and that I was being somewhat unfair to myself. Fortunately, it wasn't long before I got a welcome reality check, and it came from the most unlikely source. A few days later my soon-to-be research supervisor George Horn, a native American, confessed it had taken him around six months to get used to Australian English.

At the risk of hurting my fellow Novocastrians' feelings I will confess that my first impressions of the City of Newcastle were not entirely positive. I found it grey and dull and uninspiring – by far not a masterpiece of architectural and urban design. I will hasten to say that I subsequently came to love Newcastle very much and now consider myself a true-blue Novocastrian. I doubt that even the most devoted of Newcastle residents would fail to agree that in 30 years the city has changed tremendously, all for the better, and that it now bears little resemblance to the Newcastle of the early 1990s that I first saw.

Not surprisingly, my first days and weeks in Australia were full of new impressions, some of them positive and some not as much. By the time I had disembarked the Sydney flight around 5.30 pm it was already dark, and until I woke up on the morning after my arrival to Newcastle, I had not seen much daylight. The early onset of darkness should not have been completely unexpected given that we were in the middle of winter. But reconciling the month of July with the concept of winter did not happen immediately. Especially when on the following morning you go out the door and the most awesome sun and blue skies greet you. Oh my God! I thought I had never seen a sky that was as blue or a sun that was as blindingly bright.

Many Aussies do not fully appreciate that their days are considerably brighter and more full of light than anywhere else on earth. In subsequent years I have travelled back to Europe a number of times and I have never failed to notice how pale the sun and sky are there – that is, when there isn't a grey blanket of clouds covering them. Just over ten years ago I spent three November weeks as a visiting lecturer at a Chinese regional university in Gansu Province. I do not believe that I saw the sun even once while I was there.

The bright sun and the blue skies notwithstanding, a rather piercing cool breeze greeted me on my first day in Newcastle. The "severe" winter conditions however did not seem to bother the locals too much who strolled along the streets in shorts and thongs. I even spotted a young bloke getting off his car and walking bare-footed across the street to one of the few working cafes. Yes, it was a Saturday morning and hardly anything was open. I spent most of my first day in Newcastle exploring the Hunter Street and surrounding areas, and eventually found one of those discount stores where I purchased a few essentials, like a tea mug and a couple of plastic plates. For groceries, however, I had to wait until Monday.

Monday was also the day when I eventually headed up to the University. Until I had arrived in this country I had lived with the rather reasonable expectation that an institution called the University of Newcastle would be located in Newcastle, but Irene Hall residents soon dispelled this misconception and explained the University was in some other place called Callaghan and no, it was not within walking distance. At the risk of becoming a nuisance I will again mention that this all transpired in pre-Google times.

The bus trip from Newcastle to Callaghan was memorable in a number of ways, not all of them agreeable. When I arrived at the bus stop there were already half a dozen people there waiting for the next bus. I stood right next to the signpost and before long I became aware that I was being stared at. It was a rather uncomfortable sensation. What was going on? Did my "alien" appearance somehow intrigue them? It gradually dawned on me that they had formed something like a loose queue and that on arriving I had positioned myself right at the head of the queue.

Turning red with embarrassment I quickly moved over to the back. Much to my relief the staring stopped.

This early "cultural" experience paled in comparison with the shock I experienced when on boarding the bus the driver charged me $2.50 for a one-way trip to the University of Newcastle. I must have looked rather silly standing there next to the driver's cubicle and staring blankly at the ticket I had been issued. The guy could see me for what I was – a newcomer without a clue – and mercifully reassured me that, no, it was not a mistake, that that was indeed the bus fare to the University. How could he know that never in my life before I had had to pay more than six cents for a bus or a tram trip, regardless of its duration?

Once I had recovered somewhat from the trauma of the bus fare, the rest of trip turned into a sightseeing tour which was both enjoyable and instructional. One immediately noticeable urban feature was the completely lack of high-rise buildings. Another thing that made an immediate impression were the streets. Most of the time the bus travelled along central streets – invariably with four lanes, two in each direction. Occasionally our route took us into side streets which, somewhat astonishingly, were equally wide, even though they lacked dividing lines and were completely void of traffic. To someone like me, who was used to the tiny cramped side streets of downtown Sofia where parked cars impeded traffic even in one direction, these empty wide open side streets were a strange sight. Very much like the central boulevards, they could easily accommodate four lanes, but you barely saw a passing car. Maybe that was one of the differences between the "old" and the "new" world. When the settlers first arrived, there were so few of them and they had so much space at their disposal that they could afford having one-story residences (rather than high-rise apartment blocks) and four-lane side streets.

This urban sprawl was probably in part the reason why it took us well over half hour to reach Callaghan and the University of Newcastle where another "cultural" revelation awaited me. My concept of a university was a large building. What I found was a vast campus which, apart from a huge and presently completely empty carpark (it was the winter break!), looked more like a lovely large park than a place of scholarly endeavours.

It took me a while, but I did eventually find my way to the McMullin Building and the premises of the Linguistics Department. There I found the linguistics personnel in full force engaged in what turned out to be their regular morning tea ceremony. They welcomed me with exceptional warmth despite the fact that I hadn't bothered to forewarn them that I was due to grace them with my presence. In the midst of loquacious introductions I was handed a cup containing an insipid greyish beverage. I subsequently discovered this to be tea with milk – essentially the only way people on this continent consume tea – which turned out to be another novel and not particularly agreeable cultural experience.

On conclusion of the tea ritual the Head of Linguistics, Dr. Peter Peterson, took me to his office to talk more specifically about my studies.

Please call me Peter, he instructed me upon entering his headquarters, ignoring all attempts on my part to explain that a multi-century European cultural tradition stood in the way of addressing a senior academic by their first name.

Then he interviewed me at great length demonstrating a genuine interest in all matters relating to the life and being of one C. Moskovsky, including details of my trip and my arrival in Australia, my accommodation arrangements, my first impressions, etc. While dutifully reporting on the latter, I couldn't help but mention the difficulties I had experienced with the local variety of English.

Your long vowels and your diphthongs can be quite challenging to the virgin ear, I confessed with some unease unless it hurt Peterson's feelings. He had a laughing fit instead. I didn't know why he found my comment so hilarious, but with the passage of time my philological mind had started to capture certain phonological regularities in the way people spoke English around here. For instance, the way they uttered the word *tree* sounded a little bit like *tray*, while *tray* sounded more like *try*. An Australian version of the great vowel shift, one could say.

Not to worry, mate! my new boss reassured me. *You will get used to it soon enough. But wait until you've heard New Zealand English …*

Obviously at this point in time I was unaware that Peter was going to be my boss for many years to come. He turned out to be an exceptionally kind, considerate and supportive person, and a lot of what I managed to achieve professionally later on was due to his patient and tactful mentorship.

Over the next few days things started gradually falling into place. I was allocated a small room across the corridor to use for my studies. My own office? An unheard of luxury. I got my library card. I was assigned a cute small Macintosh computer. I had my first consultation with George Horn, my academic supervisor.

Thus commenced my scholarly journey into the intricacies of generative transformational syntax.

I did enjoy my PhD studies at the University of Newcastle very much, even in those very early days. It was an intellectually challenging, but ultimately very interesting and highly rewarding experience. I was delving in a scholarly domain, language, which I loved and whose every aspect I found truly fascinating.

I must confess, however, that outside of the world of academia my first weeks and months in Australia were not easy and that there were moments when I felt acutely unhappy. The anguish of being away from my family was such that at times it felt like my heart was going to explode from pain. I think for the first time in my life I properly understood the meaning of the term 'heartache'. But I was fully cognizant that it was not Australia that was causing the heartache.

Sure, there were aspects of the local culture and the natural environment that at least initially I struggled to adjust to – I will mention some of these in just a moment. But the people were incredibly nice to me. From Day 1 everyone without exception treated me in the kindest and most welcoming manner. The Passport Control Officer, the Customs Officer, the sweet lady at the reception of Irene Hall, the lady at International Office, all of the academic and administrative staff of the Linguistics Department. Some readers may find this hard to believe, but even officials from the local branch of the Department of Immigration (there used to be a local branch in Newcastle) treated me in the nicest possible way. It turned out that the Embassy people in Belgrade had issued me the wrong type of visa and I had to replace it. It happened overnight – no fuss at all, not even a fee.

One could say – but these were just very superficial first impressions, nothing more. This may be true, but that did not make them wrong. Indeed, very little of what I have experienced in the more than a quarter of a century residing in this country has given me any reason to change these impressions. The Aussies turned out to be an awesomely nice tribe! More about this later.

Nice as everyone was to me, I still experienced socially awkward moments – mostly due to cultural differences. For instance, I thought the locals had a real obsession with names, especially first names. The first thing they wanted to know when they met you was your (first) name and then they insisted on using it every bloody time they addressed you. The Aussies seemed particularly well-conditioned to remember names. I was not, which did create the occasional embarrassing moment when I failed to remember the name of someone previously introduced to me. It took me a while to come to recognise the cultural significance of names in the Australian (and more generally English-speaking) context. Your name is an important marker of your identity. Using your (first) name to address you is a way of acknowledging you, recognising you as a unique individual. Anything else is disrespectful.

Quite a few years later I was dating Michele, an Australian woman who had a young daughter, Sophie. One day Michele and I were talking and I asked her something about her kid. That was the expression I used – 'your kid'. Personally, I like the word 'kid'. To me, it has a nice, kind, gentle, loving sound. Much to my astonishment, Michele got really angry. *She has a name!*, Michele exclaimed. I had to muster all of my powers of persuasion to explain to her that I wasn't being rude to Sophie (whom I actually liked very much), and that Michele and I had experienced a "lost in translation" moment. Luckily, most Aussies are extraordinarily tolerant and ready to accept the cultural peculiarities of newcomers.

But what bothered me even more in these early days was the eye contact. People kept staring right into my eyes with what seemed to me like an unflinching intensity, which at times I found rather uncomfortable, verging on aggression. Again, with the passage of time I came to understand the perceived importance of eye contact – not only as a way of engaging with one's interlocutor, but also demonstrating openness and honesty.

And then there were forms and more forms and even more forms. Anywhere I went – the bank, the doctor, the International Office, everywhere, I was handed a paper form and a pen and was asked to provide various personal details. I remember that on my first day on campus I had to complete five (5) different sets of forms. What a nuisance! The good news was that in most cases you only had to do it once for the respective office or institution and then it remained there on the record.

I was particularly surprised (or should I say – displeased) with the rules that were attached to literally every aspect of life in this country. One could genuinely become overwhelmed by the rules – there were so many of them and for everything. A few weeks after my arrival there was a vacancy at one of the residential colleges on campus, International House, a much superior accommodation than my Spartan "quarters" at Irene Hall. Upon signing the lease at International House I was given a glossy brochure comprising over 30 pages of tiny print which spelled out in astonishing detail all of the things that I could or could not do as part of my residence there. Notably, the latter considerably outnumbered the former. Was this what the "free world" was really like? There didn't seem to be a lot that was free here...

To put my early frustrations with the rules in perspective, it is necessary to explain that I was not used to the type of rules-based social order that we find in many liberal democracies. This may come as a surprise to at least some readers, but in the world I was coming from there were actually very few rules. Indeed, there was only One Rule that really mattered – you must unreservedly and unconditionally obey the Government. To the extent that other rules existed, these were generally regarded as unimportant and were rarely enforced. Indeed, breaking these unimportant rules was for many people a form of tacit rebellion. We couldn't break the Big Rule – the consequences of doing so were too dire – so we broke the small rules.

Coming from such a context, it should not be surprising that I found most of the rules here disagreeable. I was also bewildered by the extent to which everyone strictly complied with them – no exceptions, no complaints – even those rules that seemed unbelievably stupid to me. Like wearing a helmet when riding a pushbike. How ridiculous!

In subsequent years I have come to realise (and appreciate) that the rules are in fact one of the most defining features of a liberal democracy. They are a form of social contract that you (symbolically) sign up for to ensure social peace and a relatively high level of harmoniousness in the way even complete strangers interact with each other. The rules ensure that people behave reasonably and do not do things which could be disagreeable, let alone disruptive, to one's fellow beings.

My (eventual) acceptance of the value of a rules-based social order notwithstanding, I find that this propensity to attach more and more restrictive rules to every single aspect of our lives has become extreme and has come at the expense of individual liberty and personal autonomy. A formidable force behind this push towards more and more rules are the country's bureaucrats – largely motivated by the desire to make life easier for themselves, not out of concern for the wellbeing of the ordinary citizen. This push is also probably at least in part driven by the obsession which the West has with safety. More and more rules are introduced in an attempt to ensure that nothing bad can ever happen to any one of us, which in some instances is taken to extremes. Regrettably, it is not just the bureaucrats that are to blame. There are also ordinary citizens – a disturbingly large number of them, in my view –

for whom individual freedom, and the personal responsibility associated with exercising it, are a burden. It is so much easier to just follow the rules. More about this later.

I know that what I will say next will upset many readers, but I have promised for this to be a totally open and sincere account of my Australian adventure and I do not intend to hold anything back. I did not like the gum trees! My initial encounter with the Australian eucalypts took place on campus. For some mysterious reason I had come with this mental picture of the eucalypt as a beautiful grand tree with a luscious crown and an imposing trunk. The eucalypt specimens that I could observe as I was crossing from the Hunter side to the Callaghan side of the campus bore little resemblance to this image. These were trees of varying height with a grayish bark and small pointed green leaves. It seemed to me that even the most benevolent observer would have a hard time detecting an attractive feature in them. Immeasurably inferior, in my mind, to the glorious mixture of magnificent oaks and pines in the old country!

Even after nearly 30 years I still do not like them. I have gotten used to them and their sight no longer bothers me. Initially it mystified me that the Aussies loved them. Then it occurred to me that the gum trees were to the Aussies what the oaks and pines were to me. And as I also subsequently discovered, most ordinary Aussies are passionately devoted and loyal to their country. Everything that is native is great, even the redback spider and the brown snake.

This was indeed a strange new world, both culturally and environmentally, but perhaps the most bizarre experience of these early days in Australia was the realisation that the sun was moving in the opposite direction. I became aware of this phenomenon one day as I was sitting in my room at Irene Hall watching a sunspot shift across the room. The sense that there was something wrong in the manner in which this sunspot was moving was so unsettling that in the days that followed I kept checking the actual direction of the sun's movement across the sky. My suspicions were confirmed – the sun was moving from right to left – in the opposite direction to what I was used to in my native land.

My brain was telling me that could not be right. I obviously knew it was not the sun that was moving. The perception of a moving sun is just a visual effect of the earth's rotation. But I also knew that my eyes were not deceiving me, either. This visual effect manifested itself in a different way down here. It took me some time to figure it out. It is all a matter of vantage point, of perspective. When you are looking at the sun in the Northern hemisphere, East is on your left. It is the other way round in the Southern hemisphere. Resolving this conundrum was doubtlessly intellectually rewarding, but the bizarreness of the sensation did not vanish overnight.

In comparison with the "wrong" direction of the sun, the "wrong" direction of the traffic in Australia was undeniably a trivial issue, albeit with potentially much more lethal consequences. The left-side traffic would unavoidably be a problem for anyone coming from almost anywhere else in the world. Earlier I briefly described the rather intense emotions which the left-side traffic induced in me on the trip from Sydney airport to the Central Station. In the weeks and months that followed I had a few uncomfortably close encounters with passing vehicles. We can become slaves to habit and I had become slave to a 30-year-old habit of looking to the left for incoming traffic first. It took a while and a considerable conscious effort to condition myself to look in both directions before crossing the street.

That aside, I found traffic in Australia to be extremely well organised and most Australians to be very disciplined, polite and considerate drivers. In the old country pedestrian crossings were among the most dangerous places to attempt crossing the street. In Australia one can do it with one's eyes closed.

As I confessed earlier, the language comprehension challenges I had to cope with on arrival were unexpected. But as my new boss Peter Peterson had predicted, I gradually got used to the Australian variety of English and was reasonably soon able to communicate successfully in most social contexts and with most Aussies. But as the weeks and months rolled on, I became aware of another unanticipated language problem. Let me explain. Around a couple of months after my arrival I found some distant relatives living in Sydney and accepted their invitation to go and visit them on the weekend. Getting to see this perhaps most famous Australian city was exciting and very enjoyable. But by far the most memorable aspect of my visit was the indescribable mixture of relief and sheer exhilaration I experienced when for the first time in more than two months, upon meeting with my relatives, I spoke Bulgarian. It was as if my soul had been shackled and all of a sudden had somehow managed to shed the chains.

Ah, to be unable to speak one's native language! Pure torture. Language is perhaps the most unappreciated trait that we, humans, have. Somewhat astonishingly, this lack of appreciation can be detected even among those who use language as their principal (and often, only) professional tool, like journalists and academics. Every one of us has an exceptionally close and intimate relationship with their native language. Is it by accident that we call it "the mother tongue"? We use it to express our most intimate thoughts, to convey our emotions, we use it to explain, to plead, to argue, to persuade, to deceive. While we can become expert speakers of another language, there are personal and emotional domains for whose expression the mother tongue remains best suited. Even after decades of life in an English speaking environment I still swear in my native Bulgarian. It is not as if I don't know the English swear words – I do. However, to me they seem to lack the emotional expressiveness of a good old Bulgarian oath.

Money matters of all sorts bothered me a lot during these early days and weeks. Starting with the physical appearance of money, I thought the coins were bizarrely shaped and enormous in size, to say nothing of the fact that the coin's size did not always correspond to its denomination. Even the texture of the notes felt strange. My new friend Barry Boettcher soon instructed me that the notes were made of plastic and were the best quality notes in the world. Knowing Barry's partiality to all things Australian, I was initially somewhat sceptical about this, but in the years that followed I came to recognise that the Aussie notes were indeed substantially superior to any other currencies I came in contact with, including the US dollar and the euro.

But the shape and the size of the Australian money were little more than a curiosity. The cost of everything, on the other hand, was a lot more than that – it was literally overwhelming. I earlier detailed my travails over the bus fare. A similarly agonised experience subsequently accompanied any purchase I had to make, with even the most basic everyday groceries costing between five and ten times more than what I would pay in the old country. Bear in mind that I had come with very limited resources and they were diminishing at a disturbing speed, regardless of how careful I was trying to be.

Money (or lack thereof) undeniably played a major role in marring my early days and weeks in Australia. Remember, in our grand design I was to find myself a job and start earning money as soon as humanly possible. And barely days after my arrival I started a sustained campaign towards this goal. I daily checked the classified in the *Newcastle Herald* and applied for whatever jobs were currently being advertised. I was indiscriminate. I was as prepared to apply for positions requiring high qualifications, e.g., language teacher, as for the most menial jobs, like supermarket trolley attendant or hospital cleaner. And I was spectacularly unsuccessful every time.

It was a particularly demoralising experience. I do not think I had ever felt such a sense of inadequacy, of impotence, inferiority – a sense of personal failure. But I was being rather unfair to myself. When my wife Violetta and I had earlier been putting our grand plans together, we obviously had been oblivious of the fact that at this point in time Australia was in the midst of its worst recession in recent history – Paul Keating's recession, the recession "we had to have". I was facing a rather harsh reality. For every job I applied there would have been scores of other, local, applicants and in this context finding a job, any job, would have been virtually miraculous. And while miracles do seem to happen every now and then (reference – Scott Morrison), my attempts to enter the Australian labour market did not produce any miracles. Meanwhile my already limited funds continued to dwindle relentlessly, regardless of how frugally I was trying to live. As the days and the weeks rolled on there was this additional pressure building on – this dreadful anticipation that sooner or later I was going to run out of money and then I would be left with few options other than pack my bags and jump on the next flight to Sofia.

Overall, with the constant heartache of being away from my beloved females and the ever growing anxiety of money pressures, these first few months in Australia were a fairly dismal experience. But it wasn't all bad. You see, while my employment efforts were floundering, my academic endeavours at the University were flourishing. After a somewhat ambivalent start due to adjustment issues and competing priorities, I was eventually able to get my studies going. I explored the theory, I started collecting language data, I had regular discussions with my academic supervisor. The project soon started to gather shape and to show real promise. Praise the Lord I had my research – it was my saving grace. It gave me meaning. It gave me purpose. It alleviated my acute sense of failure and inadequacy. I regularly spent between 60 and 70 hours per week in my little office on the third floor of the McMullin Building delving deeper and deeper into my topic. And my efforts started bearing fruit. By early October I had managed to put together a fairly coherent framework which I had the opportunity to present to the Department at one of their research seminars. The overwhelmingly positive feedback I received was very reassuring.

Indeed, my research supervisor was so impressed with my progress that he invited me to deliver a lecture on my topic to one of his third-year classes. I did spend the better part of two weeks preparing for this challenge and, judging by the student feedback I received, it was time well spent. To say nothing of the fact that I got paid at the unheard of rate of $120 for a two-hour class.

Regrettably that remained the only income that I was able to put my hands on during these early months. With my ever diminishing resources and nothing bright emerging on the employment front, by mid November I knew I had come to the end of the road. And I paid the campus travel agency a visit to book a flight to Sofia.

At this point I had no idea that only within a few months I would be coming back. For all I knew, I was going back to Bulgaria for good.

It hardly needs saying that I was overjoyed at the prospect of the imminent reunification with my family. But this joy was well intermixed with regret. People here had been so welcoming and had accepted me so warmly that I had gradually started feeling an integral part of our small academic community, and the thought of abandoning them brought along a great sadness. The genuine distress they displayed at the news that I was leaving them did not do much to alleviate this sadness.

My regret for having to leave was further exacerbated by the awareness of unfinished business. For several months I had worked extremely hard and I had become deeply engaged in my studies. I had learnt a lot. I had made considerable progress and could see my project evolving in a very exciting way. The thought of giving it up was very unsettling.

What else do I remember from these early days? Well, I saw the best and the worst of the Australian climate. I experienced the searing summer heat and the flooding rains. I had a bloody encounter with a magpie (he won). I tried Australian brandy and found it awful (to be fair, I tried the cheapest variety available in the liquor store). I tried Aussie beer and liked it a lot (still do). I also became rather partial to Australian white wine, but that happened a few years later...

Nearly 30 years later I am still here, therefore obviously that was not how our Australian adventure ended. I did fly back to Sofia, but early the following year the University contacted me to notify me that I had been awarded the University's postgraduate research scholarship. The scholarship included a generous living stipend which was just enough to meet our very modest needs. And by early March 1993 I was on my way back to Australia, with my beloved females due to join me soon thereafter.

The next few years were not without challenges. Our needs

were indeed very modest, but it was not always easy to make ends meet. Bear in mind there were four of us, two adults and two very young girls, trying to survive on what was supposed to be an individual living stipend. To give the readers a sense of how tight things were financially, we could not even afford a telephone line, let alone a car. But the social isolation was what probably oppressed us much more than the financial hardships. The Aussies we came in contact with were invariably welcoming and nice to us – I will have more to say about this a bit later – but we had few close friends and relatively few opportunities for wholesome social interactions. This level of social isolation was in part due to the fact that there were very few other ethnic Bulgarians in the Newcastle area. Shared language and culture are a powerful bond. It is not surprising that immigrants from the same ethnic background tend to flock together and form these ethnic communities – Greek, Italian, Chinese, Arabic – which provide a substitute for the social and cultural framework that the newcomers left in their countries of origin. It is an effective way of overcoming social isolation. Alas, there wasn't a Bulgarian community in Newcastle; there still isn't.

This is not to say that we were unhappy. We were together, we had a modest roof, we saw our gorgeous girls grow happy and healthy. The hardships notwithstanding, we were looking ahead and were full of optimism.

My studies at the University progressed at a steady rate and three and half years later I successfully completed my program and was awarded the highest possible academic qualification – Doctor of Philosophy. I was now Dr. Moskovsky. Shortly thereafter I had a lucky break and was hired part-time as an academic literacy lecturer at the University's then Centre for Teaching and Learning. I clearly made a very good impression, because a few months later the part-time position was converted into a full-time lectureship.

Around the same time the Centre's Director agreed to sponsor my application for permanent residence. It took us a few months to put the seemingly infinite paperwork together and in mid 1997 I lodged the application. Knowing the glacial speed with which the Immigration Department worked we braced ourselves for a long wait, perhaps years. Barely six weeks (!) had gone when we received the letter notifying us that we had been granted permanent residence. I honestly do not know if we are holding the world's record for the most quickly processed and approved immigration application, but I would be surprised if it wasn't a national record. No complaints there, obviously.

Just over two years later I was granted Australian citizenship. This occurred at a ceremony at Newcastle's Civic Hall. Then Immigration Minister Philip Ruddock was there to oversee the ceremony. He personally handed me my citizenship certificate. Seeing him at close range, Ruddock looked like a pleasant and mild-mannered man – no resemblance to the monster that most of the then media painted him as.

Towards the end of 1998 the University's Linguistics Department opened up a new lectureship in applied linguistics. I was far from unhappy with my work in academic literacy, but my heart was in language. I applied and got selected from among several candidates from around the country. And the rest, as they say, is history.

Meanwhile other good things had been happening in my family. Violetta managed to find herself a job as a surveyor at a small construction company in Maitland and started working there full-time. After spending several years confined in the home, it was a great break for her, an opportunity to again be professionally active in her field.

And of course Neda and Ellena were quickly growing up and had started going to school. We had continued exclusively using Bulgarian within the home context, but then very suddenly, barely weeks after starting school, the girls switched to English and no force in the world could compel them to speak Bulgarian. I certainly tried. Based on my professional background and experience, I was deeply convinced of the importance of preserving their mother tongue. But all of my efforts were doomed to failure. English was the language of their peers and nothing else mattered. You cannot control language.

Now that both Violetta and I had full-time jobs, our financial hardships were over. We were soon out of our Spartan two-bed flat in Jesmond and in an almost brand-new three-bedroom house in Woodberry, a small residential suburb midway between Maitland and the University. Our struggles were over.

Well, not quite, as it turned out. Real life is not a fairy tale. It very seldom has a fairy tale outcome. Just as everything seemed to be falling into place and we seemed on our way to a good prosperous life, disaster struck and my marriage with Violetta broke down. It did not happen overnight. Things between us had started deteriorating earlier and it took nearly two years before it all came to an end. How and why this happened is an extremely personal story which is well beyond the scope of this book. In the years that followed I often wondered whether this would have happened if we had remained in Bulgaria. Of course this is a hypothetical question to which no one could possibly give a satisfactory answer. There is no doubt in my mind, however, that the financial hardships we had to deal with, the social isolation, the unavailability of the support that social and family structures provide in the home environment, the challenges of adjusting to a foreign culture – all contributed to the breakdown. This is one aspect of immigration that probably is not sufficiently well understood and appreciated – immigration puts a considerable additional strain on personal relationships. My relationship with Violetta fatally succumbed to this strain and was never able to recover.

The two years during which my marriage gradually crumbled were by far the darkest period of my life, a period of considerable personal agony, of sense of catastrophic loss. The worst part is that you cannot just turn the page and start anew. Life could be so much easier if one could do that. But the reality is that the breakup does not bring the relationship to an end, not after you have been with someone for more than 20 years. So much remains that continues to tie you to your former spouse/lover/partner/mate – naturally, first and foremost your children. You feel trapped, you feel like you will never be able to put this nightmare behind you.

There was one silver lining to this relationship debacle. Both Violetta and I chose to put our children's interests first and to make every effort to ensure that our breakup would not be too disruptive and traumatic to our girls. I believe we largely succeeded in this endeavour. It was not easy, very very far from it. When a long-term relationship irrevocably breaks down, one can become overwhelmed with distress, resentment, humiliation, with a suffocating desire to retaliate, to make your ex suffer as much as you are suffering. It takes a super-human effort to suppress this destructive urge, to overcome your sense of pain and injustice and to map a constructive path forward. I take not a little pride in the fact that we managed to rise above this and to provide our lovely girls with a life which was as close to normal as our circumstances would allow us.

It took me a while to recover, but I did eventually. Time is indeed a great healer. The university job was a true life saver. I honestly do not know how I would have managed to survive without it.

My work gave me meaning, it gave me purpose, it kept me afloat.

In the middle of 1999 I presented a paper at a linguistics conference in Leiden, and once the conference was over I jumped on a plane to Sofia. It was my first visit back after we had left in 1993. Sofia looked unchanged, if somewhat dustier and messier and more pothole ridden than I remembered. The people I had left behind, family and friends, certainly seemed completely unchanged to me. For someone who was still under the emotional cloud of a recently broken marriage, the warmth of the welcome I received was immensely uplifting. Six years after the start of our Australian journey, Bulgaria still felt like home to me.

Popular wisdom tells us that it takes the average immigrant around ten years to adapt to the new conditions and to start to belong. It took me a bit longer than that. In the second half of 2005 I spent several months on sabbatical at Sofia University. It began well and was fun for a while, but then I started to feel increasingly restless. I noticed that I was growing increasingly frustrated with all kinds of things in the old country – social, cultural, political – but particularly people's attitudes. I also noticed, with not a little surprise, that I was missing my life back in Aussie land. By the end of the sabbatical I was raring to go back. The flight back was uneventful save for one experience which I still remember as vividly as if it had only happened yesterday, not nearly two decades ago. My itinerary involved switching flights at Jakarta airport. When I arrived at the respective boarding gate for the Sydney flight there were a bunch of people there speaking in the unmistakable Aussie accent. It literally warmed my heart to hear true Aussie speech. At this moment I knew it was home I was going back to!

Interlude 1:

On Nationhood, Ethnicity, Race(ism), (White) Privilege, etc.

I will start this chapter with a heretical thought. Different nations/ethnicities are not all the same. Mind you, I am not suggesting one ethnicity is superior over another – this would be an awful proposition and one which is unsupported by any credible evidence. All I am saying is that, historically, different nations/ethnicities evolve in different ways and because of that each forms a distinct set of social, cultural, psychological, etc., features. To me, this point is so glaringly obvious that it seems absurd to argue against. Take, for instance, the European nations. Start from the North and move down South and then go further East. How can anyone reasonably argue that the Irish are the same as the English or the Scandinavians or the French or the German or the Spanish or the Italian or the Serbian or the Greek (and so on and so forth)? And we can only be eternally grateful that we are all different. Can you imagine how unbelievably boring life would have been otherwise?

Lovers of English literature would be familiar with the work of Jerome K. Jerome. The all-knowing Wikipedia describes him as "an English writer and humourist, best known for the comic travelogue *Three Men in a Boat*", published in 1889 – a hilarious account of the adventures of three young Englishmen rowing a boat up the Thames. About a decade later came *Three Men on the Bummel*, which details the same protagonists' travels around Germany. Most of the book is about the main characters' shenanigans in a foreign country, but towards the end there is also an essay-like chapter devoted to an exploration of the German national character. It is an amazingly insightful and profound portrait of a national psyche which is inherently and uniquely German – a psyche which was on global display in the following decades.

The note above is less about Jerome's brilliance and insightfulness and is more about something else. Even the most brilliant mind cannot capture something that does not exist. Jerome captured a uniquely German national psyche, because there was/is one. Different nations and ethnicities do have distinctly different social and psychological profiles. Their existence is what has given rise to quite well-known respective national/ethnic stereotypes. No reasonable person would deny that stereotypes are simplifications and that it is very wrong to treat individual people on the basis of a stereotype. But neither should we be blind to the fact that stereotypes do capture prototypical features of national/ethnic identities.

When in the middle of the 1990s my dear friend Barry Boettcher retired after a long and distinguished career as a Professor of Biological Sciences, he and his wife Moira undertook something akin to a world tour, with the idea of visiting every place to which they had a connection of one sort or another. Much to my excitement, their itinerary included a week or so in Sofia where Barry had a long-standing professional associate. When they returned a few months later, I paid them a visit. I was curious to learn about their Bulgarian experience. One thing that Moira said struck a (jarring) note with me. *If only the Bulgarians could smile a bit more*, she suggested. It was such a hurtful thing to say, or so it seemed to me at that time. A few years later I went back to visit the old country. The opportunity to reunite with friends and family was a joyous one, but I was also noticing things to which I had not paid too much attention before, including the undeniable scarcity of smiling faces. We, Bulgarians, are a morose lot. To be fair to my fellow Bulgarians, I think Australians (and Westerners more generally) tend to smile too much, even when they are not in a particularly smiley mood, so approximately half of the time their smiles are confected and insincere. But then, what do you prefer – a sincere frown or a fake smile? I think I will go with the fake smile.

One could think of different nations/ethnicities as different individuals with different personalities, each involving a unique combinations of features – some more extrovert, outgoing, optimistic, spontaneous, friendly, helpful, generous, etc.; others – more composed, more reserved, less outgoing, less forthcoming; yet others – greedy, jealous, vindictive, unforgiving, etc.

(Think of the difference between an Aussie airhostess on a Qantas flight and a German airhostess on a Lufthansa flight. Both are exceptionally professional, courteous and expedient, but when the Aussie smiles at you, her smile warms your heart. When the German lady smiles at you, it leaves you cold.)

We are living in very unusual times when some of the most fundamental concepts – the very essence of our understanding of what the world around us is like – are being challenged, re-defined, even denied. There is no objective reality out there, there is no objective truth. Everything is a matter of our subjective perception and is shaped according to our purely emotional response. Empirical evidence is utterly irrelevant. If we do not like the evidence, we simply ignore it or deny its existence – even if centuries of research and scientific exploration stand behind it.

The first time I came across this phenomenon was in the mid-noughties. I was working with a graduate student on a project examining the role that language aptitude plays in the acquisition of a new language. Language aptitude can be described as a type of intelligence which is specific to the learning of second/foreign languages. In simple terms, high aptitude means that the minds of some learners are better equipped to capture the system of the new language, and such learners typically learn at a faster rate and achieve a higher level of competence in the new language. The psychological reality of language aptitude has long been recognised – both by researchers and language teaching professionals. Specialised aptitude tests, which have been in existence for around a century, have shown a remarkable capacity to predict subsequent success in second language learning.

In an earlier part of my professional career I worked as an English instructor at a very large language teaching institution in Sofia, with regular student intakes in the hundreds. Some of our new students were complete beginners. Others had previously learned some English, some of them a lot. Before each term we ran a battery of diagnostic tests, including a fairly rigorous aptitude test, in order to place our new students in relatively homogenous groups. Teaching staff competed fiercely among each other for the best performing groups, for a very simple reason – high-performing students are easier to teach. Paradoxically, the greatest demand was not so much for the students with an already good command of English, but for the complete beginners who got the highest scores on the aptitude test. We knew from experience that by the end of the term these beginners invariably outperformed everyone else, even the students who had started with plenty of previously acquired English competence.

Imagine my astonishment when I read in an academic source that language aptitude is not a valid concept, because it is "undemocratic" – it arguably bestows "unfair" advantages on some, while disadvantaging others. The term "cancel" had not yet come into existence at that time (not in its current sense), but you get the idea – someone wanted to cancel aptitude, because it offended their sense of fairness, because it disagreed with their moral principles.

When someone pointed out to Alexandria Ocasio-Cortez that she had gotten her facts wrong, the outspoken American Congresswoman famously declared that (I am paraphrasing) she did not mind being factually incorrect as long as she was "morally right". AOC was deservedly ridiculed for this statement on some conservative media. True, at some superficial level it is a very silly (and, therefore, funny) thing to say. At a deeper level, there is nothing funny about it. What AOC said is actually terrifying, because it implies that there can be a morality which is unaligned with empirical facts, a morality which is completely detached from reality. A morality which a very vocal minority on the left (of whom AOC is a prominent representative) relentlessly demand from the rest of us to accept, whereby abandoning the tremendous amount of knowledge about the world around us derived through centuries of often brilliant scholarship. How can anyone in their right mind believe that anything good can emerge from this?

Concepts undeniably grounded in empirical fact and which for centuries have universally been regarded as unequivocally valid have not been spared. 'Man' is no longer 'man', and neither is 'woman'. There are no physiological or psychological differences between men and women, we are all the same. Biological sex is completely irrelevant and meaningless. Gender is a socially determined construct and purely a matter of personal choice. One can choose to be male in the morning and female in the afternoon. Or any one of scores of other "genders" that no one had heard of until five minutes ago.

All cultures are the same, all ethnicities are the same, all races are the same. To suggest anything else is an awful thing, a manifestation of racism.

I am an old-fashioned guy. I believe in science. I believe in the existence of an objective reality which can be empirically established. I am aware this has become a heretical view, but I am not prepared to abandon it. To abandon it would amount to abandoning reason and sanity – in other words, it would amount to giving up the very essence of what makes us human, of what sets us apart from any known other species.

In the forthcoming chapters I will express some other "heretical" views which the proponents of the new "thinking" will undoubtedly denounce as racist. Everyone and everything that does not conform to this unthinking new ideology is branded as racist. White people are racist by virtue of being white. Any attempt to deny that you are a racist only reinforces your inherent racism. Established empirical facts are racist, statistics are racist, mathematics and biology are a form of white supremacy. The term 'racist' has become so diluted that it has practically become devoid of meaning. Unfortunately this loss of meaning has not reduced its power to condemn. To be branded as racist, no matter how unreasonably or unfairly, can completely destroy your life.

As a linguist (and as a reasonable human being) I care about meaning very much, which is why I am going to define the meaning of the term 'racism' and work on that basis. I doubt my definition of racism will impress the new social justice warriors, but I will do it anyway – for my own peace of mind if for nothing else.

As part of working on this short chapter, I reviewed the definitions of 'racism/racist' in a number of online reference resources. According to the Cambridge Dictionary, 'racism' is "the belief that people's qualities are influenced by their race and that the members of other races are not as good as the members of your own, or the resulting unfair treatment of members of other races," while 'racist' is defined as "someone who believes that other races are not as good as their own and therefore treats them unfairly." In a similar vein, Merriam-Webster tells us that 'racism' is "a belief that race is the primary determinant of human traits and capacities and that racial differences produce an inherent superiority of a particular race."

These definitions are representative of what one typically finds about racism in such reference resources. Racism is commonly defined in terms of negative attitudes to members of another race, including a belief that they are inferior solely by virtue of being members of that race. Another commonly emphasised aspect of racism concerns unfair treatment of, and/or discrimination against, individuals or groups on the basis of these individuals' racial characteristics.

In a broader sense, racism involves the formation of attitudes to a person or a group solely on the basis of their being a member of another race. Such attitudes may or may not be externalised in any obvious way. Mind you, I am not saying it must be a negative attitude – it could well be a positive one. As long as this attitude, negative or positive, emerges solely on racial grounds, it is a form of prejudice and a manifestation of racism.

I have come to the view that there are roughly three categories of racists. There are individuals who harbour a negative prejudice to another race or ethnicity, and as a result often treat their members unfairly, including instances of (negative) discrimination. This type of racism is obvious and easy to identify. Its effects on the community where it occurs are so profoundly negative that the need to unreservedly oppose it requires no justification whatsoever.

Another type of racism is not as obvious, because it (arguably) involves positive attitudes to another race/ethnicity. In most cases, these attitudes are sincere and are typically rooted in a desire to rectify actual or perceived injustices historically inflicted on the members of a particular race. Such attitudes have often been the driving force behind the establishment of various government and non-government agencies and the introduction of various social and cultural policies whose principal aim is to support racial/ethnic communities which have historically been subject to racial abuse. A noble cause, no doubt. But given that it is solely based on racial grounds, it is in its essence racist.

One could reasonably argue – so what if it is racist, as long as it brings about good, as long as it improves the targeted group's wellbeing? But does it really? Does positive discrimination produce the outcomes which it was intended to? Various forms of positive discrimination have been in place quite extensively for several decades already in most of the Western world, particularly in countries with established racial minorities like Australia and the USA. It is an unpalatable truth for many, but the reality is that these policies have not improved, by any objective measure, the lot of the people that they were intended for. Quite the opposite seems to be the case. The evidence suggests that these policies have been instrumental in entrenching victimhood and welfare dependency among these communities, in essence depriving them of agency.

There is also a relatively small (but extremely vocal) section of the community who take the position that suggesting anything even remotely negative about an ethnic or a racial group, regardless of how factually accurate this may be, is a form of racism. An obvious example is the higher incidence of domestic violence in some Indigenous communities – something which is empirically well established and documented. Dare to say anything like that and you will immediately be slammed as racist. But if we genuinely have these communities' wellbeing at heart, how can not talking about the social and cultural issues that seriously diminish their wellbeing be helpful? How can you address a problem if you choose to remain silent about its existence?

It is also worth pointing out that those who are the most vocal and militant advocates of minority groups' welfare never produce any meaningful ideas in relation to how established inequality can be resolved. Their ideas (if we could call them that) never go further than vacuous symbolism and are completely impotent to improve the lot of the people they are presumably intended to help.

Assigning people a joint identity (e.g., as members of an ethnic or racial group) is divisive and counterproductive. It diminishes us as unique individuals and takes away our dignity. Treating people solely on the basis of their ethnic or racial identity inherently assumes race/ethnicity to be *the primary determinant of human traits* (check the Miriam-Webster definition of racism above). It entrenches racism rather than contributing to its elimination.

Given the imperfect human condition, it is unclear to me whether one could reasonably hope to eliminate racism altogether, although it would certainly be possible to marginalise it to an extent that would make it virtually irrelevant. Based on what I have witnessed here in the past three decades, Australia had come very close to achieving this. How? By treating everybody as an individual, with respect for, and consideration of, their personal circumstances, completely disregarding their race or ethnicity or even culture. Now an increasingly pervasive identitarian ideology, with its unhealthy obsession with race and ethnicity, is turning the clock back.

I am mindful that what I have done above is a futile exercise, especially as far as the social justice warriors are concerned, and that I will be slammed as racist regardless. Let me tell you about my "racism" then. My professional career evolved in a way which brought me into contact with students representing a vast array of different cultures, ethnicities and races. The academic programs I have delivered have involved large numbers of international students coming from almost everywhere around the world – Asia, the Middle East, Africa, Europe, North America, Latin America. Some of these were graduate students doing research under my supervision. With most of them I formed very close bonds. With some I formed a lasting friendship. Not a single time in my career have I noticed any indication, direct or indirect, that any of my students have experienced a negative, let alone discriminatory, attitude from me. Indeed, quite the opposite is true. Over the years I have had volumes of largely unsolicited feedback conveying students' appreciation of the training and guidance they received from me, appreciation of the time, care and attention I have given them. Two rather extreme examples of former students' manifestation of gratitude are worth mentioning. After completing his doctoral program under my supervision, Chen (not his real name) returned to China and established an English language school for children. Chen called the school *Christo*. I was unaware of this until a few years later I was shown pictures of the School, with my first name on display on almost every vertical panel around the place. It was touching, but at the same time excruciatingly embarrassing. One of my earlier Saudi PhD students came back to Australia for a conference nearly 10 years after he had completed his program. Tariq (not his real name) contacted me and said he wanted to catch up, and we arranged a meeting. I didn't realise then he had flown to Newcastle specifically for the meeting (the conference was elsewhere) and that he was due to fly back to Saudi Arabia on the same day. We spent some time together chatting and, on leaving, he gave me a small gift-wrapped package. I only unwrapped it after he had disappeared and was utterly stunned by the generosity of the gift – at a guess, worth a few hundred dollars. My first instinct was to rush after him and give it back. Then better sense prevailed. I knew he would never accept it back and an attempt to return the gift would only deeply humiliate him. By the way, Tariq is not an

Australia: Early Days (and Beyond)

unimaginably rich Saudi prince, just a humble academic.

Over the years I have developed an essentially a human-centric approach to life. In my philosophy of life, people's wellbeing should take precedence over everything else. A human being is more important than sharks, or lizards, or spiders, or trees. Cultures are important, but human beings are more important.

If a decade or two ago someone had told me I would become a fan of Trotsky, I would have died laughing. As I relatively recently learned, Trotsky famously said: *Increase the power of man over the natural environment and abolish the power of man over man.* What a remarkably nice idea! Unfortunately for around half a century or so already we have witnessed the opposite trend – an ever growing subjugation of the individual to largely imagined environmental issues and an ever increasing size and power of governments.

A very destructive ideology has been infecting most of the Western world in recent years promoting the idea of "white privilege", of some imagined oppressive patriarchy mostly perpetrated by white men. It is an ideology which has elevated race as the primary (if not only) determinant of all social relationships.

This obsession with race provoked some self-reflection in me. It occurred to me that until quite recently race had never been a part of my self-awareness, never been a relevant identity dimension, that until quite recently I had never thought of myself as belonging to a particular race. I proudly say that I have never thought of the people in my professional or social environment in racial terms, either. I found people agreeable or disagreeable for what they were like as a person or for what they did or didn't do – not because they were black or white.

I cannot, however, deny the undeniable – I am male and I am white. I could argue that I am not the archetypal white guy, being a mixture of Balkan, Middle-Eastern and Slavic ethnicity, but I am undeniably Caucasian. A white male … Not a good combination nowadays. Being a white male has elevated me to the top of the patriarchal hierarchy wielding oppression onto everyone else. Being a white male has automatically granted me incomparable advantages over anyone else and has bestowed me with immeasurable privilege. So let me tell you about my white privilege.

I can divide my "privileged" life into two almost equal halves. My early privilege occurred in the first 30-odd years of my life under the "tender" care of the Bulgarian Communist Party. What my "privileged" life in Bulgaria was like was covered in some detail in an earlier chapter. Then I moved to Australia in order to continue a life of privilege. For over three years my family and I (= two adults and two charming kids) occupied a tiny flat consisting of two bedrooms and a miniscule kitchen; the latter also served as our living room. For three and half years we did not have a phone or a car. We could not afford either – the four of us were living on an individual stipend (my scholarship). For over three years my wife and I slept on a mattress on the floor (we didn't have a bed).

Yes, things improved a bit thereafter. My lectureship paid me a decent wage, enough to ensure we have a roof over our heads and to put food on the table. Once I started having a regular income, I was able to purchase a second-hand vehicle (thank you, CBA, for providing the loan!). Quite a few years later I took another (much larger) loan to buy my modest home; I am due to finish repaying my home loan by the age of 70 (provided I am still alive). I never owned a brand-new car until I was nearly 60 years old. I was already in my early 60s when, for the first time in my life of privilege, my bank deposits shyly nudged above my debts. Mind you, a paper-thin margin, but finally in positive territory and, for someone who utterly abhors debt, something to rejoice.

The "privileged" life I have described above is in no way exceptional. Quite the opposite – based on what I have seen or heard, my "privileged" journey in Australia is not dissimilar to that of many other migrants. I remember my first landlord Pando (Paul, for his Aussie mates), an ethnic Macedonian. By the time I met Pando, he and his Macedonian wife and their two kids had been running a fish and chips takeaway shop at Charlestown for over 20 years. He once told me that they (including the children when they were a bit older) typically worked at the shop 12-14 hours a day, six days a week. A life of privilege indeed. At one point Pando took a loan and purchased an investment property, then another one, then a third one. He was not 50 yet when, by his own admission, he and his family had managed to accumulate over a million dollars. Another privileged white male millionaire, no doubt.

The idea that people like Pando and myself are part of some privileged oppressive hierarchy is not only patently wrong, it is diabolically evil. It more than anything shows the profound absurdity of what has regrettably become mainstream left-wing ideology.

3

The Quiet Australians

So where are the Aussies on this spectrum of nationalities/ethnicities? What is the prototypical Aussie "persona" – nice or nasty, friendly or hostile, generous or stingy? The answer to this question can vary dramatically depending on who you ask.

"Australia is deplorably racist," proclaims Jack Latimore in *The Guardian* (10 August 2018). I have picked this title quite randomly. Latimore is by far not a lone voice in denouncing ordinary Australians as racist. Most of the mainstream media, including radio, TV and newspapers, abound with negative assessments of Australia's national character. And it is not only the media – quite a few Government and public institutions gleefully indulge in the same. If you pay attention to the media (as I do, the glutton for punishment I am), Australians are not only racist – they are intolerant, bigoted, chauvinistic, homophobic, xenophobic, islamophobic, misogynistic, you name it. The media keep unrelentingly piling on about the ongoing "epidemic" of domestic violence (which is a cover term for men bashing their wives), about an "entrenched rape culture" on university campuses, about our alleged cruelty to refugees. It all makes Australia and Australians look like an appalling pit of awfulness.

I could go on and on – there is enough scope here for not one, but several books. But this is not what this book is about. Its purpose is to describe as truthfully as possible my personal experience of life in Australia, my own impressions of the Aussie tribe. And I will wholeheartedly declare that after nearly 30 years of continuous residence in this wonderful country I have seen very little evidence of the awfulness that keeps pouring out of almost every media outlet. Indeed, the complete opposite is true, in my experience at least. I found ordinary Aussies (the "Quiet Australians") to be extraordinarily friendly, tolerant and accepting – perhaps more so than any other nation on earth. I can confidently state that they are considerably more tolerant and accepting than my fellow Bulgarians. Based on what I have seen and read and heard, Europe is literally ridden by xenophobia, islamophobia and racism. Racial and ethnic intolerance is deeply entrenched in so many parts of the world today, including Asia, Africa, and Latin America. One would have to search far and wide to find a nation whose people are as decent and as tolerant and as welcoming as the Aussies.

Did you know that, with 42% of residents born overseas, Sydney has the largest mixture of ethnicities anywhere around the world? Compare this with New York (29%), Paris (22%), Berlin (13%), Tokyo (2%), Shanghai (<1%) (*The Weekend Australian*, 2 February 2020, Bernard Salt). The happy, peaceful and prosperous co-existence of Sydney residents in and of itself completely invalidates all claims of racism and bigotry.

Do you remember the Sumatra tsunami in 2004? This monstrous tsunami hit a number of places around the Indian Ocean, but it was Indonesia's Aceh province that incurred the greatest damage. Approximately 131,000 people were confirmed dead and 37,000 missing, more than 80,000 houses were destroyed, more than 500,000 people were displaced on Sumatra alone.

In a word, it was a human tragedy of biblical proportions. I remember how deeply affected I was by the way the Aussies responded to the disaster. Credit goes to John Howard's Government for unconditionally giving Indonesia one billion dollars in aid. But impressive as that was, it almost paled into insignificance by comparison with the response of the ordinary men and women of Australia, the "Quiet Australians". They gave unsparingly, unreservedly. Donations poured in in the millions, but much more impressively they gave their time, their service, their professional skills. So many of them – doctors, nurses, engineers – dropped everything, their families, their homes, their jobs, their comfortable and nicely ordered lives, and were on their way to Indonesia. They went there to provide critically needed assistance little of which was available locally. Many of them remained on Sumatra for weeks and even months helping the local communities get back on their feet. I watched in awe.

Quite a few years later in a conversation with my sister back in Bulgaria I was describing the kindness and generosity of Australians, probably best exemplified by their response to the tsunami disaster. Ah, my sister said, but it is easy to give money (to help others) when you are rich. It was not much of a sacrifice, in her view. Whether being rich in and by itself makes people generous is doubtful. I imagine that being well-off makes it easier, but it is not a sufficient condition. It takes kindness and generosity of spirit to donate to others. Importantly, the Aussies did a lot more than give money. As I detailed above, many Australians, especially from the medical profession and from various emergency services, packed a hasty bag and jumped on first available flight to Indonesia so that they could go and help complete strangers in another part of the world, in a disaster region, in a place of chaos and destruction, with all the associated risks to their health and even their lives.

It is impossible to reconcile the harrowing narratives in the media with the observed reality. Take the alleged inequality of women in Australia, the claim that Australian women are constantly being mistreated (including physical abuse) and discriminated against in various ways, that they are tormented by their husbands at home and are sexually harassed at the workplace and elsewhere, that they are being underpaid (in comparison with males), etc. Nothing can be further from the truth. One of my first impressions shortly after arriving in this country was the remarkable level of liberation and empowerment of Australian females compared to what I had previously experienced in my own country, Bulgaria, which – for all of its flaws and deficiencies – is a European culture with an arguably strong tradition of gender equality. These first impressions were so powerful that I wrote about them in a letter to a former senior colleague and mentor in Bulgaria, Professor Dr. Andrey Danchev (now deceased). In that letter I wrote: "The Australian society has achieved female emancipation. Women in this country are extraordinarily liberated and empowered, in some respects even more than men." I wrote this in the early 1990s.

To avoid being misunderstood a note of clarification would be in order here. I am **not** suggesting that the Australian society is completely free of any racism, bigotry, discrimination, gender bias, etc. That would be an utterly unsustainable position. I have read credible stories of racially prejudicial attitudes in the past – usually, but not only, towards Indigenous Australians. I have heard credible stories of very recent acts of racism/bigotry. A few years ago I had two gorgeous girls from Changchun in China's North doing my masters program at the University of Newcastle. They once confessed to me that some young idiot had called them a nasty racially charged word as they were walking to the shopping centre. One of my fabulous Saudi research students was out with his wife and his two young children. They are religiously very devout and his wife had the full Islamic veil on. And again there was some idiot who called them a nasty word and told them to "go home". So – yes, there are idiots here too, no doubt about that.

It can be a hard pill to swallow, but that is reality. We are all human and therefore imperfect – morally and ethically and psychologically. Anything else is utopia, a pipe dream. Wherever there are human beings there will be some level of bias, prejudice, racism, bigotry, discrimination. Regrettably, this seems to be an essential part of the human condition. But as with almost everything else, the critical issue here is one of degree, it is all relative.

To digress somewhat from the topic, one of the things I found rather surprising in my early days in Australia was people's propensity to complain about living costs. **Everything** was soooo expensive! Bearing in mind that that was taking place in one of the richest countries in the world, it was rather difficult for a newcomer to take these laments seriously. "Expensive" is not an absolute term – the nominal cost of a product/service is relatively immaterial. The fact that a kilogram of apples in Australia costs between five and ten times more than in Bulgaria is largely meaningless. What matters is how much of a product/service an average consumer can purchase on their weekly income, and the reality is that Australians' purchasing capacity is several times higher than almost anywhere around the world.

Whenever I was exposed to this type of rhetoric I always felt the urge to challenge my interlocutor to give me an example of a less expensive country than Australia. I rarely did – I was too keen to avoid showing disrespect for the nation that had treated me with so much kindness and had offered me so much hospitality. But it is a legitimate question.

The same reasoning should apply to the issues discussed above. Every time we hear these allegations of racism, sexism, bigotry, etc., we need to ask the question – which other nation on earth is freer of racism, sexism, bigotry, etc., than Australia? To prove this point, let me offer the reader a simple quiz. Please consider the following question and choose a single answer from the list below it:

Where would you prefer for your daughter(s) to be born and raised?
   a) Albania
   b) Australia
   c) Bolivia
   d) Bulgaria
   e) Ethiopia
   f) Ghana
   g) Greece
   h) Haiti
   i) Kyrgyzstan
   j) Mexico
   k) Sudan
   l) Saudi Arabia
   m) The Philippines
   n) Uruguay
   o) Venezuela
   p) any other

If you have picked up anything other than (b), you are either an utter hypocrite or an idiot.

My early impressions of the societal position of Australian women turned out to be very accurate and everything I have seen since has reinforced them. When considered with reference to women's position elsewhere, Australian women are among the most privileged and liberated females in the whole world. Indeed, there is growing evidence that the balance of dominance may already have tipped in favour of females and that males are increasingly the subjugated gender in Australia (and perhaps more widely in the West).

In fact, there are credible voices claiming that what we, in the West, are currently witnessing is not merely a simple shift in the juxtaposition of the sexes, but also a real crisis of masculinity, with dire implications not only for men, but for women as well. Some of the data which US academic Dr. Warren Farrell presents in his most recent book, *The Boy Crisis*, are quite sobering. Everywhere in the developed world boys are falling behind girls in every single academic subject, especially in reading and writing (these two are the biggest predictors of future success or failure). We have seen a strong growth in mental health issues for boys/men, incl. depression and suicide. Did you know that 20-24 year-old males are five (5) times more likely to commit suicide than females in the same age group? Boys are also four times more likely to become addicted to opioids; they suffer from much higher rates of obesity; higher school truancy; stronger tendency to drop out of school; higher rates of unemployment; much, much higher rates of imprisonment (93% of the prison population in the USA are males). While this all has been transpiring, political and media elites have relentlessly been piling on "toxic masculinity", misogyny, domestic violence, etc. Enough, please.

The story of the "awfulness" of ordinary Australians is a myth, it is fake news. Do not trust it – trust your eyes and your common sense instead. In my nearly 30 years of life here I cannot recall a single case in which I was mistreated or abused for being an alien, an immigrant, a newcomer. The complete opposite is true. From Day 1 in this country I have been treated with great courtesy, good nature and good humour. Again and again I have seen people going out of their way in order to be helpful, regardless of whether this was the Passport Control Officer, or the Customs Officer, or the receptionist at the medical centre, or my Departmental Head at the university, or my neighbours. Or even the bus driver.

Let me tell you about the bus driver. It must have been in the year 1993. Our younger girl Ellena was barely a toddler. On weekends we sometimes took the bus from Jesmond to Newcastle and spent the day on the beach; the girls loved playing in the sand. One day we were returning from our beach holiday and midway through our bus trip home Ellena indicated a pressing need to pee. What a disaster! Interrupting our bus trip meant we would have to wait an hour for the next one, to say nothing of the unaffordable bus fare! Be that as it may, it seemed we had no choice here. The bus was at a stop and was just about to take off when I approached the driver and somewhat embarrassed explained our predicament and asked him to let us get off. Without a word he flicked the door switch and the four of us disembarked. We attended to young Ellena's relief on a convenient patch of grass nearby. As we turned around to return to the bus stop I noticed with some amazement that our bus was still there, door open, waiting for us! The bus driver beckoned to us, again with a completely expressionless face, to get back on the bus, as we did. None of the handful of passengers on board expressed any displeasure at the unnecessary delay. In fact I could see a few smiling faces. It may be hard to find a more quintessential example of the profoundly decent nature of ordinary Australians.

To those who ceaselessly decry Australia's awfulness I have a simple proposition – it is a big world out there, go and find a less awful place to live in (but before you do that, perhaps have another go at a slightly amended version of my quiz above).

If there are worrying trends taking place among ordinary, especially younger, Aussies these have nothing to do with racism or bigotry or xenophobia, etc. Phenomenal prosperity in combination with a mind-blowingly generous social welfare system have conspired to breed at least two generations of young Australians many among whom are a bit spoiled and unprepared for hardship, unwilling to put in any substantial effort for their own advancement. Unfortunately, parents and educators have played their part in that. It never ceases to amaze me that Australia has to import labour from overseas, because there are jobs which the locals are unprepared to do themselves – even if they are currently unemployed. The local boys and girls are clearly too precious (and comfortable enough on the dole) to go pick up fruit in the outback.

I still remember with astonishing clarity how stunned I was when very early on – must have been 1993 or 94 – a young man in his late teens or early 20s openly told me that he was living on the unemployment cheque and that he had absolutely no intention of doing anything about that. He just wanted to have fun, he told me, go surfing, have a few drinks with his mates. The dole was not much, but enough to cover his most essential needs. *Why would I enslave myself in a job stuck behind a bloody desk 40+ hours a week when I can be out having fun all day, every day*, he asked rhetorically. It did not occur to him to ask himself a somewhat different question, viz. where is this (dole) money coming from? It did not even seem to cross his mind that he was living the life of a parasite, that other people had to put in the hard work so that he can have his fun.

But harsh as my words are, I am not placing the blame solely on the youth. I rather think that we, as a society, have betrayed them. Overprotective parents and a misguided education system have failed to instil in them proper values, the dignity of hard work, the importance of living a life with a purpose. I see more and more of this type of attitude – especially among younger Australians – a sense of entitlement, a belief that the world around them owes them, that the world around them is somehow obligated to ensure their own happiness and wellbeing. Now this is a trend that should really have us worried.

Mind you, I am not suggesting we should be despairing. All I am saying is that there are valid reasons to be worried and that that is an issue which deserves a lot more to be in the centre of public attention and subject to public debate than the plethora of completely meaningless and inconsequential social and cultural causes pursued by the progressive elites.

It is not all bad with the younger people in this country by any measure. There are lots and lots of them who are committed, hard-working, aspiring for the future. Let me tell you about Mitch, the grand nephew of my bridge partner (and deeply loved friend) Pam. I had mentioned to Pam that I needed some electrical work done at my place and she referred me to young Mitch, a licensed electrician in his mid 20s. I literally fell in love with this young man. Tall, charming, gentle, soft-spoken, extremely courteous and stunningly competent and expeditious. Mitch arrived at my place around 4 o'clock one afternoon after a full shift (which had started at 6 am) and worked like a possessed person for another four and a half hours. He cleaned up before he finished and left with a few hundred honourably earned dollars in his pocket. Pam tells me Mitch recently took a home loan to purchase a run-down property which he is currently renovating mostly by himself, in his spare time. We do not need to worry about Mitch. He is truly on his way. Thank God for the Mitches of Australia! Not all is lost.

I have to finish this chapter on a personal note and there isn't a better way of doing this than by a brief note of thanks to a handful of extraordinarily decent Australians who have played a prominent part in my Australian adventure. They certainly do not come more decent and generous than Barry and Moira Boettcher.

If they had been my own blood parents they could not have been nicer or more helpful. A very remote Bulgarian connection led us to them and the Boettchers effectively adopted us from Day 1 and have treated us with no less love and care than they have for their own four children (all of them also great Aussies!). Thank you, Moira! Thank you, Barry! A day rarely goes by without thinking of you with love and profound gratitude.

When we first arrived, we settled in a small flat in Jesmond. And we very soon met our next-door neighbours Gail and Lawrie, an Aussie family with two children, Adrian and Lareina, approximately our children's age. You could not find more ordinary Aussies (in the best sense of the word 'ordinary'), a perfect example of ScoMo's "Quiet Australians". Gail and Lawrie took us under their wing and went out of their way to help us in any conceivable way. They were not well off. They were renters, like us. Gail worked as a low-paid courier. Lawrie was on a disability pension – he had a range of serious health problems including a weak heart (which gave up a few years later, may his soul rest in peace). Regardless of that we were regular guests at their modest, but immaculately kept home. They helped us adjust to a new environment, to become part of their social network. Neda and Lareina started school together at the local primary school. Gail and Lawrie entertained us, they took us to see places in and around Newcastle. Gail would leave their two kids with Lawrie and would take the four of us on sightseeing tours in their small Holden. It was through her that we first discovered the beauty of the Hunter Valley, Patterson, Dungog, Chichester Dam, you name it. Lawrie was taken from us before I got a chance to give him my heart-felt thanks. I am very glad I have had an opportunity to do so with Gail. She is now a neighbour living in her own little house barely a few hundred meters from my own place. We regularly bump into each other on the street and chat, and one day I mustered the courage to remind her of our early days and the immeasurable good that she and Lawrie brought into our lives then. I wanted to make sure she knows we had not forgotten. My confession brought tears to her eyes.

And then there is Phillip, one of the kindest and most generous persons I have ever met, a true gentlemen (forgive this old-fashioned word!). Phillip (now a retiree) had a rather busy job as a building inspector, but he nevertheless took time to assist newly arrived refugees with improving their English language skills. But he did not feel sufficiently competent in that role and took up a postgraduate program at the University of Newcastle in order to build his English teaching expertise! This is the type of person my friend Phillip is! And that was how we met – in the mid-noughties he was one of my students. We very soon became good friends. We still are. Phillip was the person who reunited me with the game of bridge (I had not played for 20 years or so) and was thus instrumental in bringing a new and valuable social and intellectual dimension to my otherwise rather secluded life. When I turned 50 Phillip conspired with my two daughters to set up a surprise birthday party for me and a select group of friends at a fancy restaurant in Newcastle. And he stunned me by footing a bill which easily ran in the high hundreds (perhaps more).

Speaking of bridge, I joined the Newcastle Bridge Club in the mid-noughties and started playing regularly once or twice a week. My dear friend Pam is a bridge veteran and one of the Club's founders half a century ago. An awesome old lady and a formidable bridge player – most players shudder when she comes to take her seat at their table! Pam must have seen something in me (although I often wonder what) and chose me as one of her regular bridge partners. What a humbling honour! And for well over 10 years already she has loyally stood by me – on and off the bridge field – and has put up with my less than perfect bridge manners. I love her with all of my heart.

In early 2005 my girls and I moved into our newly purchased home in a small residential suburb of Newcastle. And we soon met our next-door neighbours, Marie and Neill – two of the most decent people I have known, true salt-of-the-earth Aussies. What a coincidence, one could say – first Gail and Lawrie, now Marie and Neill. Well, it is either a coincidence (and I am the luckiest guy in town) or it's just that Australia is blessed with an abundance of Gails and Lawries, and Maries and Neills. Coming across one or two of them does not require an exceptional stroke of luck. It isn't luck, but it has certainly been a privilege to have had Marie and Neill's ongoing friendship, support and good humour. I came to live with the rather comforting confidence that whatever help I found myself needing, I would get it from them. Neill was a retired army man. The poor man passed away a few years ago after a surgery-related health complication. Marie, in her 80s, recently succumbed to cancer. It was heart-warming to see the amazing amount of love and support her family extended to her. May her soul rest in peace!

This narrative will be incomplete without acknowledging the broader neighbourhood of my place of residence where people have made me feel particularly welcome, have given me a true sense of belonging. I am out usually twice a day doing the rounds with my faithful companion Buddy – a proud representative of the Dachshund breed. Literally everyone we see says hello to us, invariably with a warm smile and a good word. As we go along the suburb's streets, I regularly see arms stretching out of the windows of passing cars to greet us. Most of my neighbours know my first name and never hesitate to use it. Somewhat embarrassingly, I don't know the names of most – it's just that that was never a part of the old culture and my mind was never conditioned to remember names. It does not seem to bother them. I am aware that I cut an eccentric figure – the goofy foreign professor with the sausage dog! It does not seem to bother them, either. Quite the opposite. They never miss an opportunity to show me that they fully accept me, that as far as they are concerned, I am one of them. It is heart-warming.

Interlude 2: On Communism, Socialism, Capitalism, Liberal Democracy, etc.

In a previous chapter I described how in my earlier life in Bulgaria I admired and even envied Western capitalism. We idolised the West for its industrial might, for its advanced science and technology, for its artistic creativity. But above everything else, we admired the West for its democracy and its freedom, for the way liberal democracy had been able to empower the individual. In the same place I also confessed that having now spent nearly 30 years in one of the most advanced democracies in the world (Australia), my admiration of liberal democracy has subsided somewhat. Apart from anything else, I found it to be a surprisingly clumsy system. Social and economic reforms occur at a glacial pace. I can appreciate the need to take considerable care in planning and implementing change – not least because of the perils of unintended consequences. But it can take an eternity for even modest reforms to occur. And when a bad law or regulation comes into place (as they do!), it could be next to impossible to get rid of it.

And of course, capitalism is also ridden by a plethora of other problems, such as corruption, inequality, crime, drug addiction. Most of these problems are so plainly in sight that even capitalism's most ardent proponents would not try to deny their existence. It is an imperfect system, no doubt about that. But what is the alternative?

The critics of capitalism are numerous and very vocal. They are remarkably accomplished at identifying the problems (real or imagined), although they rarely offer practical and/or productive solutions to these problems. Many among them take the view that the system is so deeply and inherently flawed that it is virtually irredeemable, therefore we need to replace it. Some of these critics remain notably silent about what the putative replacement would look like. They call for the dismantling of the institutions on which capitalism and liberal democracy are based, with the completely unfounded belief that whatever comes into their place has got to be better.

Others openly advocate for socialism as the only viable alternative to capitalism. From the perspective of someone who has experienced first-hand the "blessings" of life in socialism, such advocacy seems bizarre (to put it mildly). These people have chosen to remain willfully oblivious of the monstrous socio-political experiment which took place over the past century in so many places around the world. It started in Russia in the early part of the 20th century and in the middle of the century spilled over into parts of Asia and Eastern Europe. We subsequently saw offshoots in Africa (Zimbabwe) and Central America (Cuba). And if the 20th century is "ancient" history for the proponents of socialism, we have had a very recent (and ongoing) example in Latin America (Venezuela).

The results of this experiment, regardless of where geographically it took place, have invariably been profoundly bad – a comprehensive social, political and economic failure. You need not look further than Germany and Korea – the two divided nations where this experiment had its quintessential manifestation. East Germany vs. West Germany (before the reunification) and North Korea vs. South Korea. Same nation, same people. One half unbelievably successful, prosperous and free; the other half immeasurably poor, destitute and unfree.

The Venezuelan socialist experiment is also worthy of a brief note. Venezuela used to be one of the economic crown jewels of Latin America. Trivia buffs will tell you that Venezuela is more oil-rich than Saudi Arabia. Yet in under 20 years Hugo Chavez and his political descendants were able to turn this lovely country into a complete basket case, a country whose people have reportedly been reduced to eating their pets to avoid starvation. It takes a special "talent" to turn the Saudi Arabia of Latin America into one of poorest and most destitute countries in the world.

The evidence is there, glaringly obvious for anyone to see it – if they wish to see it, that is. When one tries to point to socialism's admirers that history abounds with examples of the failure of socialism to produce anything but abject poverty and misery for its people, they say – *but that was the "wrong" type of socialism, we want to build the "right" "good" type of socialism*. Somewhat predictably, they are (again) disconcertingly vague about what the "good" socialism looks like. When one presses them to offer real-world examples of places where the "good" socialism has been accomplished, they invariably point to the Scandinavian countries and say – there you go, I rest my case!

But are countries like Norway, Sweden and Denmark actually socialist? The answer to this question clearly depends on how one defines "socialism". According to the Marxist doctrine, socialism involves public ownership of the means of production. Put simply, this means that the state owns and controls all businesses, all factories, all agriculture. Private property is strictly limited to owning your place of residence (typically a tiny apartment in a high-rise block) and a small patch of land to grow some fruit and vegetables for your own consumption. And even this very limited private ownership is largely meaningless, because it can be taken away from you at a whim.

The Marxist conception of socialism quite obviously fits what we saw in the Soviet-style socialism everywhere it occurred. It certainly does not fit the alleged Scandinavian socialism. It therefore appears that what the advocates of the Scandinavian-style socialism have in mind is rather different from the Marxist conception. They rarely care to articulate this clearly, but perhaps their idea of a socialist country is one which involves a very generous and very comprehensive social welfare system. But by this definition Australia is also (already) a socialist country, because it does have a very generous and very comprehensive social welfare system. One could reasonably debate whether our system is as good as what they have in Sweden, etc., but no one can reasonably deny that it is considerably more generous and comprehensive than almost anywhere else around the world. In essence, if this is the type of "socialism" they have in mind, relax – we already have it here in spades.

It actually seems to me that the attempts to invent a Scandinavian model of socialism are essentially disingenuous, designed to obscure the discussion and to deflect from the political left's fascination with the Soviet type of socialism. Those who are even vaguely familiar with 20th century history know how much support (both tacit and vocal) there was for the Soviet Union and affiliated states (like Cuba) among the West's political left. This support was perhaps partially understandable in the very early years of the Soviet state, at a time when still not much was known about the regime's atrocities. But with the passage of time the true nature of the regime started coming out in graphic and very confronting detail. Continuing to support Soviet socialism in the face of so much unequivocal evidence of its evilness was profoundly immoral and inexcusable. Yet there is plenty of it even now. It was, for instance, quite astonishing to see prominent representatives of the left (like Canada's Justin Trudeau) openly grieve the passing of Cuba's murderous dictator in 2016. Let's also not forget that not too long ago the political left in the West (including here, in Australia) celebrated the rise of Hugo Chavez and socialism in Venezuela. They have been conspicuously silent about the "merits" of the Venezuelan model of socialism more recently.

I remember how in the earlier years of my residence here I was profoundly bewildered by the largely benign attitudes that many people here (especially in academia) took to historical figures associated with Soviet-style socialism, including Marx and Lenin and Fidel Castro (to mention just a few). I vividly remember how stunned I was when at a humanities research seminar I saw an image of Marx proudly displayed on the final powerpoint slide of the presentation. The topic of the seminar actually had very little to do with Marx or Marxism, and it seemed as if the picture of the "great" ideologue was simply inserted there as a political statement on the part of the author. I soon realised that that incident was not a statistical outlier, that it was not a one-off act of an eccentric (and deluded) academic. Quite the opposite – I started to have this haunted feeling that I was constantly surrounded by images of Fidel Castro, Che Guevara, even Lenin – on posters, on portraits, on t-shirts. But how can that be, I never ceased wondering. These were profoundly evil men, mass murderers in the most literal sense of the word. I felt a perverse sense of relief that I was not seeing any images of Stalin or Mao.

These attitudes completely baffled me, at least initially. I could see strongly held beliefs against fascism/naziism, a profound condemnation of the evils of fascism. I could see these anti-fascist attitudes across the whole political spectrum, not only on the left. Yet when it came to Soviet socialism, I could detect very little condemnation – certainly none on the part of the political

Left. But how could that be? Were these people willfully blind? Surely, on the backdrop of a century of history it is impossible not to realise that Soviet socialism/communism is as evil as fascism/naziism.

For anyone who bothers to give these issues more than a passing thought it would be glaringly obvious that fascism/naziism and Soviet socialism/communism are strikingly similar in so many ways. Did you forget what the acronym 'nazi' stands for – National **Socialism**?

Let us take a brief detour along (Bulgarian) history lane. Zhelyu Zhelev was the first democratically elected President of post-communist Bulgaria. Before that Zhelev was a Philosophy Professor at Sofia University, whose book *Fascism* (1982) turned him, perhaps unwittingly, into a dissident. The book was conceived as an academic study of the nature of fascism as a totalitarian socio-political order. Barely three weeks after the book came out in print, the communist authorities banned it and it was removed from all book stores. The reason? Someone high enough in the communist hierarchy read the book and found that the picture it painted of fascism was disturbingly similar to what took place in the equally totalitarian communist world. And Zhelev became a dissident overnight.

The findings in Zhelev's book should hardly come as a surprise. The two types of regime may represent the extreme right and the extreme left, but in terms of the nature of the regime and its practices they are strikingly similar to each other. Both involve a totalitarian dictatorship, brutally repressive enforcement agencies (think – *Gestapo*, *KGB*, *Securitate*, *Stasi*), complete lack of civil rights and freedoms, merciless punishment of any real or perceived act of subordination, including jail, concentration camps and even physical annihilation. Both are responsible for inflicting immeasurable poverty, misery and death on their population.

But while in qualitative terms fascism/naziism and Soviet socialism/communism can be seen as equally evil, quantitatively Soviet socialism/communism easily leaves fascism/naziism behind. This can clearly be established by looking at the number of each regime's peace-time victims – in other words, the number of people who lost their lives as a direct consequence of the actions (or inactions) of the State, not as war casualties. In the former Soviet Union alone, the regime's peace-time victims are estimated anywhere between **20 and 80 million** people (this is according to Russian sources). China in its turn "contributed" another 100 million or more, especially during Mao's "cultural revolution". How many other lives socialism destroyed elsewhere around the world is anyone's guess, although it will again be in the tens of millions at least.

The peace-time victims of fascism/naziism – however we choose to calculate their number – would be considerably fewer, perhaps by orders of magnitude.

Someone said – we only learned one of the two big lessons of the 20th century, that of fascism/naziism. The lesson of socialism/communism has remained unlearned.

Churchill is credited for the statement that capitalism/democracy is a very imperfect system, but is superior to any of the others we know of (or something to that effect), although I am not sure whether the great man bothered to articulate in what ways capitalism is superior. Several decades later in a public critique of the Communist Manifesto Jordan Peterson did exactly this – explained why/how capitalism is superior. All forms of government – socialism, capitalism, monarchical absolutism, etc. – produce inequality. According to Peterson, the nature of the hierarchies underlying social order in all kinds of societies makes some inequality unavoidable. But capitalism is the only system which also **creates wealth** and it does that for **all** of its citizens, including the socially lowest and most disadvantaged classes. Then Peterson goes on to cite some United Nations data showing that in the last 200 years the income of the poorest members of society has grown by between 300 and 400 percent and that thanks to free market capitalism the world is on the verge, for the first time in its history, of eliminating absolute poverty.

One of the favourite maxims of capitalism's critics – that *the rich are getting richer and the poor are poorer* – is not based on actual fact. Under capitalism, *the rich are also getting richer and the poor are also getting richer.*

Please, let us recognise the lessons of the 20th century and abandon the astonishingly absurd idea that there is "good" socialism. There is no more "good" socialism than there is "good" fascism/naziism. Please, let us finally put this folly behind us.

4

The Loud Australians

Affluence is good, poverty is bad. This seems like a thoroughly uncontroversial view. How could anyone possibly argue that being poor is better than being rich? Based on my experience living in Australia, however, I have come to the view that being very affluent for a very long period of time can be bad for the soul. It makes you lose a sense of perspective, a sense of what really matters.

The wise and worldly protagonist painting of Hannah Rothschild's bestselling novel, *The Improbability of Love*, shares a similar view: "the moment people become rich and achieve their earthly desires they enter a painful, spiritual vacuum."

I am certainly not preaching for the virtues of poverty. Real poverty – especially extreme poverty, when daily life is reduced to a mere struggle to survive – is debilitating, punishing, diminishing, disempowering, denying personal dignity. I have not seen much evidence of such poverty in Australia. This is not to say that there aren't many people here whose income is limited to their weekly wage and who would regularly struggle paying the bills. But even with them, existence is not reduced to a mere struggle for survival. For many of these people, having to get up early every morning, take the kids to school, go to work, do the shopping on the way back, cook dinner, do the laundry, clean the house, mow the lawn, etc., may be a burden, but it gives them a purpose, it provides meaning. If Jordan Peterson is right, having meaning is the most important thing in life – more important than happiness (whatever the latter means).

There is a sizable section of the Australian community who are very affluent and who have been affluent for a very long time. They do not have to get up early in the morning in order to go to work. They do not struggle to pay the bills. Many of them have nannies looking after the kids and cleaners taking care of the household. Nothing wrong in that, I suppose, but then how do you fill up the 24 hours of your day? What do you do with your life?

In essence, prolonged affluence can gradually remove the sense of purpose in one's life and take away its meaning, especially in a context in which religion (Christianity, in particular) plays an ever diminishing role in our lives.

But we can't live in a vacuum and once the burden of the daily chores disappears, we go and try to find purpose and meaning elsewhere. We go out searching for a purpose, for a mission. Nothing wrong in that, either – unless it is a mission which may seem morally admirable, but which requires no effort, no personal sacrifice, and which in practice does very little to address the issue which, on the face of it, this mission is about.

In search of a moral cause many members of our affluent class tend to take up fashionable social justice issues which require little or no effort or personal sacrifice on their part. They would advocate for the rights of (failed) asylum seekers, but would never consider hosting a refugee family in their own (secluded) mansions. They will call for action on global warming, but without spending a single dollar on solar panels or an electric vehicle. All gain and no pain.

It would not be too difficult to find numerous examples of wealthy individuals embracing a social justice cause which enables them to claim the high moral ground at no personal expense or sacrifice. One that stands out, in recent times, is Sydney celebrity Dr. Karen Phelps. Dr. Phelps chose to become an advocate for the rights of the asylum seekers on Nauru and Manus Island, and was the principal force behind the now discredited Medivac bill. Notably, embracing such a cause did not in any way stop Dr. Phelps from taking up two elected positions – one on the Sydney City Council and one in the House of Representatives in Canberra, neither did it interfere with her multi-million dollar GP practice in Sydney. Phelps is clearly a highly competent and experienced medical professional. Someone with Dr. Phelps's noble profession can make a genuine difference in ordinary people's lives – for instance, by spending a few years in one of the remote Aboriginal communities and exercising her professional skills there. But that would have a very disruptive effect on her lifestyle, wouldn't it? Producing loud noises about asylum seekers is so much easier. Makes you feel good about yourself and costs you virtually nothing.

Much of the same is on display among the political, media and academic elites in Australia. A preoccupation with fashionable virtues, an obsession with often completely vacuous symbolism. Like branding Australia Day as "invasion day" and calling for its cancellation – presumably as a way of rectifying current and historic injustices allegedly inflicted on Australia's Indigenous people. Very few among these activists seem to ask themselves the question – how would changing or even abolishing altogether Australia's national day make any difference to the lives of Indigenous people? How much would it alleviate deep-rooted disadvantages, especially in the remote communities? How much would it improve their living standards, their health and education? How much would it make the life of a single Indigenous child happier? Would it stop the epidemic of Indigenous teenage suicides?

It should not take a brilliant mind to know that renaming or even cancelling Australia Day will make absolutely no difference to any of the above. Such rhetoric is pure poison, it is very divisive, it sows mistrust between different sections of the community, it has the potential to tear the fabric of society.

Unfortunately, many of these social justice activists are not only very affluent, but are often also in societal positions of great power and influence. Many of them possess extraordinarily powerful platforms – in the media, in the parliament, in public institutions, in academia – which they relentlessly use to pursue their agenda. I think it is high time that we, the quiet Australians, found our voices, high time that we stood up to them and called them out.

Now let me turn my attention to the political class specifically. Alas, I will not have too many nice things to say about our pollies. Indeed, the opposite will be the case. Few other aspects of life in this great country have given me so much disappointment, disillusionment, resentment and even contempt.

To put my attitudes to Australia's political class in perspective, I will have to briefly return to my earlier, pre-Australia, life. For obvious reasons, in conditions of communism there isn't much politics going on (if any). There was no political pluralism, no competing political parties, let alone competing ideas. Every aspect of life was run, top-down, by the Party nomenclature. On the backdrop of this, it was fascinating to see political life in the West as depicted in the movies or to read about it in books.

In Chapter 1, I described the enormous amount of admiration that in these days we had for the West – not only for its prosperity, but also for its unparalleled achievement in science, art, technology. This admiration extended to the West's politicians. Remember, an iron curtain divided us from the West, and because of that we were unable to observe the minutiae of Western politics. The late 70s and most of the 80s of the last century, however, were dominated by two political giants – Margaret Thatcher and Ronald Reagan. No iron curtain could obscure their political prominence or diminish their global significance. I do not think I can adequately describe how much I admired Thatcher and Reagan. To the oppressed nations of the Soviet Bloc, they were a source of hope and inspiration. At a time when the "Empire of Evil" remained strong and apparently indestructible, these two political trailblazers uncompromisingly stood up to it and eventually were instrumental in bringing it to its knees. Central and Eastern Europe owe a lot to Ronnie and the Iron Lady for their liberation from Soviet rule in the late 80s and early 90s of the last century.

Thatcher and Reagan were my benchmark for conviction politicians, for leaders prepared to take the hard road for their values, rather than the comfortable path of political expediency. Unfortunately for Australia's political class, Thatcher and Reagan were the benchmark I brought along when I came to this country.

Having arrived in Australia in the early 1990s, I only caught the tail end of the Hawke-Keating era. In fact, I didn't get a chance to see Bob Hawke in action, although by all accounts he was one of Australia's political giants, a truly remarkable leader. No one seems to dispute Hawke's imposing legacy, no one denies that Australia owes much of its current prosperity to his Government's reformist agenda.

I did see Paul Keating in action. I found him a bit arrogant, but undeniably very capable as a politician, with a formidable presence in the chambers of Parliament. The then Liberal opposition seemed to cringe whenever Keating stood up to speak.

I had barely been in the country a few months when the 1993 election took place – the "unwinnable" election, as it came to be known. This clash of political wills that evolved in front of us was a fascinating political spectacle. We had Keating's relentless campaign against John Hewson's rather dull and uninspiring performance. I also witnessed first-hand the amazing power of negative campaigning. I still remember these seemingly incessant political commercials on every TV channel showing the rising costs of everything arguably due to occur as a result of Hewson's proposed goods and services tax. Clink, clink, clink – up goes the price of cars, TVs, fridges, you name it. And it clearly was very effective, because a triumphant Keating was returned for another three years. But in time the Australian public had had enough of him and by 1996 had their metaphorical baseball bats ready for him.

I dabbled in political activism at the 1996 election. My friend and mentor Barry Boettcher decided to run on behalf of the Australian Greens for the seat of Newcastle. And he asked a bunch of friends, myself included, to help with his campaign.

I will not hide that I was rather troubled by Barry's political choice. By then I had already acquired a fairly good idea of what the Greens stood for and what in essence they were like. I have subsequently come to regard them as the most destructive force in Australian politics and social affairs more generally. When I first started paying attention to Australian current affairs, I had the sense that the Greens' rhetoric sounded uncannily familiar. I soon came to the startling realisation that they sounded exactly like the propaganda machine of the communist regime in Bulgaria. Sure, the themes they explored were seemingly different, but the tenor of their rhetoric was essentially the same: grandstanding, vicious, unrelenting, uncompromising, peddling glaring untruths. There is little doubt in my mind that their crazy conservationist policies blocking land management and fuel reduction have been ultimately responsible for the intensity and scale of the bush fires we have experienced in recent years. They presumably pursue these policies to protect the native fauna and flora. But the fuel on the ground keeps building up and up, and when a fire unavoidably gets going (this is Australia) it burns with such ferocity that it is virtually unstoppable. And the environmental damage (to say nothing of scores of human lives lost) exceeds by far the (arguable) environmental loss caused by reasonable land management and hazard reduction practices.

But my views of the Greens notwithstanding, I was doing this for Barry. Nothing was off limits for him. I would have been there by his side if he had been running for the Australian Communist Party (luckily extinct by then). And I knew that he deeply cared for the Australian environment (and everything Australian), clearly being one of many harbouring the delusion that the Greens are about the environment.

Barry certainly had no illusions about the minor party's chances of winning in Newcastle, a Labor stronghold. He chose to run regardless, because he was convinced that political pluralism is good for democracy, that having another player alongside the Labor and the Liberal monoliths will strengthen Australia's democracy and will make it healthier. That's the kind of person Barry Boettcher is.

Just as the 1996 campaign was due to start, Barry gathered his troops to organise the logistics and allocate tasks and resources.

Each member of his taskforce was assigned a couple of residential districts. Our mission was to distribute campaign brochures and other promotional materials as widely as possible. I will confess that I was very sceptical whether a glossy piece of paper with a dozen pompously worded statements on it could change anyone's voting intention. But I embraced my mission regardless. I was doing this for Barry and was determined to help him as unsparingly as I could.

If my memory is right, I had Lambton and North Lambton allocated to me. For the following two weeks or so I was out every morning with a bagful of campaign materials, and – one by one – I dutifully covered every street in these two suburbs. I may have missed a letterbox or two, although I doubt that. One thing I still vividly remember was the bewildering variety of letterboxes – different sizes, different heights, different construction materials, different widths of the aperture. I thought – God have mercy on the posties!

On the day of the election I manned one of the local voting stations (at a local school). I spent around ten hours there handing out how-to-vote cards. Compared to the passions of recent elections in post-communist Bulgaria, this was a very tame and dull affair. And I say this admiringly. The more stable and established a democracy is, the less eventful elections are.

At the end of the day I was back home, welcoming the opportunity to put my feet up and enjoy a glass of chilled Australian sav blanc. The election results soon started rolling in and before long it was clear that the Australian public had not held the baseball bats back. Keating was gone and Australia had a new Prime Minister – John Howard.

On the following weekend Barry had set up a thank-you barbeque party for his campaign troops in Blackbutt Reserve. It was the typical sumptuous Aussie affair, with mountains of sausages and rivers of beer. At one point Barry took the floor to express his gratitude for the work we had done for him. He also read out a detailed break-down of the election results suburb by suburb. The data were pretty uniform across the whole Newcastle region, with the Greens winning around 5% of the vote. With one exception – in Lambton and North Lambton the Greens had grabbed 8% of the vote. Still single digits and not particularly impressive in absolute terms. But the 3% difference actually represented a 60% rise in the Greens vote compared to elsewhere. And we all know that most Australian general elections are often won or lost within margins smaller than 3%.

I am not sure what else the Greens' better performance in Lambton and North Lambton can be attributed to other than the determined legwork of yours truly. It taught me a valuable lesson. Determined campaigning does make a difference. My earlier scepticism notwithstanding, even something as plain and simple as putting a glossy campaign brochure in people's letterboxes can make a difference. This seems to be a lesson that many of our current crop of politicians, especially on the right, have forgotten or have never learnt. I think compulsory voting has made many of them lazy and complacent, has conditioned them to take the voters for granted. Compulsory voting has taken away the need to go out and clearly articulate their program to the public, to try to persuade them, to try to win their confidence.

John Howard, Australia's Prime Minister for the next 11 years, was anything but lazy and/or complacent. Very down-to-earth, very humble, but a rare conviction politician all the same, one who was prepared to stand up and defend the values he espoused. Indeed, in the eyes of many conservatives, Howard remains the gold standard of contemporary conservatism. Many adore him and have as much regard for him as for the great Robert Menzies himself.

Such attitudes to John Howard are not at all groundless. His was undeniably an extraordinarily successful Government. And there is absolutely no need to take such assertions on faith – the facts speak for themselves. Howard took the reins at a time when the country had barely started to recover from Keating's recession, and presided over unprecedented economic growth. By the end of the Howard "reign" in 2007, unemployment was at just over 4% – lowest in more than 30 years, the average Australian was **twice as affluent** as they had been 11 years earlier, wages had grown by 20% (real growth, adjusted for inflation), and 80% of the population either owned the home they were residing in or were in the process of paying off the mortgage. All national debt had been repaid and the country had a very healthy bank balance. Not a bad legacy by any standard.

Much as Howard deserves to be admired for his Government's considerable achievements, we should not remain blind to a number of (in my humble view) serious political errors he made. To my best knowledge Howard was the leader who first introduced middle-class welfare. These were in effect handouts (disguised as tax benefits) mostly to middle-class individuals and families who were not in dire financial straits by any flight of the imagination. These handouts were essentially dishonest, a form of electoral bribery. But that aside, once such entitlements enter the system it is virtually impossible to get rid of them. No politician ever dares to touch them, because they know that a merciless electoral punishment will follow. But just imagine how much Australia would have benefited if all of this spending had gone into health and education or infrastructure?

In the wake of the Port Arthur massacre in 1996 Howard

introduced his draconian gun laws. Admittedly, he did this as a way of responding to the completely understandable public outcry prompted by the monstrous crime committed in Port Arthur. But by doing so, Howard in effect punished tens of thousands of decent and law-abiding gun owners for the crime of a single man. It was a very illiberal thing to do. Perhaps even more importantly, by doing so Howard sent a powerful signal that it is OK to suspend or even remove established rights and freedoms, as long as there is a real or perceived crisis. And this has been an ongoing trend all along since then, reaching a disturbing climax during the pandemic when most of the state leaders started behaving like totalitarian dictators brutally suppressing even the most basic freedoms of their people. For someone who loves freedom, seeing protesters being beaten or even shot at in the street (with rubber bullets, but still…), seeing people get arrested for posting a message on Facebook has been immeasurably disconcerting. More on this topic in a further segment of this book.

Howard was a cautious, but certainly not timid politician. He was prepared to make hard decisions (e.g., on illegal immigration) and to undertake difficult economic reforms. He was fully mindful of the risks involved in introducing the goods and services tax, which nearly cost him his political life.

"Work choices", a boldly conceived reform of the Industrial Relations system, which came later in his term in office, may have been the last nail to Howard's political coffin. I am not being critical of the PM's attempt to inject some flexibility into an archaic and unbelievably rigid IR system and to at least partially relieve its strangling grip on the economy. I am critical of the way in which this failed reform was handled. By the time these events unfolded, Howard had already been at the helm for a good 10 years and for the first time in living memory had managed to achieve political control over both houses of Parliament. I think this made him a little too confident, a little too complacent. I think he had started to lose his acute political judgement.

Howard should have known that the proposed reforms were a tad too radical for the Australian public's taste. A somewhat more moderate and incremental reform would have had a considerably greater chance of success. And he and his ministers should have been out there persuading the public of the need for such a reform, rather than saturating the air with cynical taxpayer-paid political commercials that were ubiquitous on every TV channel.

Howard is particularly vulnerable to criticism for the last 12-24 months of his tenure. His rivalry with Peter Costello is well known. Howard had been able to manage this rivalry very skilfully and to maintain a stable and united Government. This was reportedly achieved at least in part on the back of a verbal agreement with Costello that Howard will pass the reins over to him at a particular point in time in the future. It did not happen. Howard reneged on his commitment. I don't know what he was thinking. In the final year of his tenure he can't have not known that his Government was doomed, that the Coalition were going to be slaughtered at the upcoming election. Yet he chose to stay on as PM. He obviously found himself unable to overcome his ego and quietly step down as leader six months before the polls or even earlier. That would have been the right thing to do – for the country, for his party, and not least for his own sake.

At the 2007 election Howard ended up losing his own seat – the one he had held for I don't how many decades. A rather humiliating end to an otherwise very distinguished political career. I am sure he wishes that he'd taken leaf from John Key – arguably New Zealand's most successful Prime Minister ever – who in 2016, after 8 years at the country's political helm, stepped down on his own accord at the height of his success, with nothing to mar his remarkable legacy.

Would the 2007 election have evolved differently with Costello as the Liberals' leader? In view of the then prevailing electoral moods, a radically different outcome seems unlikely, but we will never know, will we? One thing we did know even then – with Howard as their leader the Liberals did not stand even a remote chance of winning.

One last thing about Howard before we turn our attention to his successors in the PM seat. What was he thinking when he chose to promote Malcolm Turnbull's political career, to immediately give him an important cabinet position, to press him to stay in politics after Turnbull lost the leadership in 2009? Surely a sound judge of character like John Howard should have known better. Or was he just trying again to outmanoeuvre his principal challenger Costello by positioning another leadership contestant on the board? Promoting a man like Turnbull was wrong regardless of the motivation behind it. It is hard to imagine that Howard is oblivious of the fact that a bit later his protégé came disconcertingly close to destroying Howard's beloved Liberal Party.

We have had quite a collection of Prime Ministers since the Howard era. None of them could faithfully be described as a great leader, indeed most of them demonstrated rather poor leadership. Kevin Rudd stands out as a rather disturbing combination of an appalling human being (on the testimony of his own parliamentary Labor colleagues) and an appalling leader. I still remain confused about why/how he was able to capture the public's imagination and to be so spectacularly popular in his day.

Malcom Turnbull comes a very close second. Turnbull has been painted in (some of) the media as a hugely narcissistic, petty-minded, and vindictive person, but that is unimportant. Much more important was his complete inadequacy as a leader. It is still a mystery what Turnbull wanted to achieve once he managed to grab hold of the coveted Prime Ministership – that is, other than remaining in this position for as long as humanly possible. There certainly wasn't much evidence in the way he behaved as Prime Minister to show he had a vision, a dream for the country which had given him so much opportunity and had made him so rich and successful. I wonder what he believes his legacy is – the man who (nearly) destroyed the Liberal Party?

Julia Gillard was quite popular while she was the Deputy. After she took over from Rudd, she was never able to shed the shadow of knifing a first-term Prime Minister. Then her turn-about on the carbon tax further diminished her stature in the eyes of the voting public. People knowing her personally describe her as a very nice, warm and charming person. I have no reason to doubt that, although I do doubt that even her staunchest supporters would claim Gillard was a great Prime Minister. And if some do – what do they have to show for their claim? Gillard does deserve credit for the dignified way in which she exited politics and has behaved since then. We can only regret that some of the other ex-PMs have not taken leaf from her book.

Tony Abbott was, and remains, a darling of the conservative right, although he was never popular among the general public – either as opposition leader or as Prime Minister. Yet anyone knowing him on a personal level claims that he is a remarkably nice and decent human being – honest, highly principled, extremely loyal. His decision to keep Peta Credlin as his Chief of Staff in the face of relentless pressure from many of his own cabinet ministers is sometimes cited as an example of his loyalty.

A number of high-profile commentators have expressed the view that keeping Credlin was a major destabilising factor ultimately contributing to his removal as PM. To what extent this was really the case is difficult for an outsider like me to say, but there is another angle to this story that seems to have escaped the public's attention. We elect our politicians to be exclusively loyal to us, the general public. We do not care at all whether Tony, Kevin and Julia are loyal to their spouses, friends and political allies. They have a duty to be loyal to us. If Abbott's loyalty to Credlin did contribute to the destabilisation of his Government and the subsequent fiasco of the Turnbull years, his decision to keep her was an act of disloyalty to us, the general public. (To avoid misunderstanding, I have nothing but respect and admiration for Credlin.)

Regrettably, this is by far not the only criticism I have of Abbott and his Prime Ministership. In my view, essentially the only area in which Abbott manifested strong leadership was border protection. Whether you agree or disagree with the policy, no one can deny that his Government (with then Immigration Minister Scott Morrison) was spectacularly successful in stopping the boats at a time when there was a virtual consensus in both political and media circles that it cannot be done. The fact that Abbott was able to do that is a good example of the extraordinary powers that governments have – powers so great and wide-ranging that there are very few goals that governments would be unable to accomplish, as long as they choose to pursue them and have the will and the determination to see them through.

The sad reality is that most contemporary politicians have neither the vision, nor the ambition to pursue difficult issues. The quagmire of the Indigenous people in this country is the most glaring example. Even remotely approaching its resolution would require strong leadership, conviction, unrelenting determination. Instead, as with so many other complex and challenging social and cultural issues, our "leaders" prefer to tread water while the problems become more and more entrenched and increasingly more difficult to solve.

In light of our politicians' general apathy and lack of desire to tackle difficult problems, Abbott undeniably deserves credit for choosing to take on a very challenging problem, illegal immigration, and for having the will and determination to see it through. Harsh as it may sound to his supporters, I do not believe he deserves credit for much else. I will leave aside the completely unwarranted spending commitments he made just 48 hours before the election – at a time when it was glaringly obvious even to the most disengaged observer that the Coalition will win the 2013 election in a landslide. While making these commitments was just plain stupid, breaking them within a few months was nothing but reckless – effectively conceding the moral high ground on which he had won the election (when he in part campaigned on the importance of keeping promises).

His lack of leadership was also on particular display in relation to reining in government spending and balancing the budget – what was then framed as "budget emergency". Whether calling it "emergency" was an exaggeration or otherwise is relatively unimportant. For anyone with even a remotely conservative streak, issues of government debt, budget deficits and fiscal discipline are of considerable importance. A country's budget is obviously immensely larger and more complex than a family's budget, but the fundamental principles of managing it are essentially the same. Regardless of how rich a nation or a family is, there is a limit to disposable money and it needs to be allocated wisely. Importantly, if you choose to allocate more to one item (say, the age pension), it will have to be at the expense of another item (e.g., health care). Debt is a normal, perhaps even economically necessary, part of most budgets, but it needs to be kept within manageable limits, because when it gets out of control it will sink you – regardless of whether you are a private individual or a whole state.

But issues of government debt, budget deficits and fiscal discipline are not just a matter of plain economics. They have a moral and ethical dimension. It just isn't right to spend money that you do not have. It is very wrong to encumber our kids and grandkids with debt – for no other reason than because we lack the discipline and integrity to live within our means.

It deserves to be noted that in the period leading up to the 2013 election and in the Abbott Government's early days in office, fixing government spending and balancing the budget was flagged as one of the Government's key priorities – right alongside "stopping the boats" and "axing the (carbon) tax". But then it somehow disappeared from the Government's agenda – at least the agenda that was out there in the public domain – only to reappear barely weeks prior to the Government's first budget.

The budget involved a range of spending cuts which predictably caused a massive outcry not only from affected interest groups, but from the general public as well. Were the proposed spending cuts so draconian to justify the public's negative response? A number economists (admittedly, mostly right of centre) have argued that the proposed budget measures were in fact quite moderate and reasonable, and perhaps did not even go far enough to properly address the problem. But if they were right, why did we get such a strong negative response from the Australian public? This is a complex question which warrants a longer discussion and is unlikely to have one simple answer. Some commentators have suggested that many Australians have become rather used to John Howard's "middle-class welfare" and were loath to have their entitlements taken away. While there is probably a grain of (grim) truth in this, there was, in my view, one other critical factor which substantially contributed to this outcome. The Australian public were **psychologically unprepared** for spending cuts, regardless of how moderate and reasonable these may have been, and that was because there was no one to prepare the public – political leadership had completely gone AWOL.

Regardless of what you may think of Tony Blair's leadership, even his most ardent critics will not deny that he was perhaps the most successful British Labour leader in at least half a century, a conviction politician who was prepared not only to stand by his views, but also to go out and try and persuade the general public to follow him. In a 2010 interview to National Public Radio in the USA Blair famously said: "I think if you're a politician you need to be able to know how you can shape public opinion… **Politics is a business of constant persuasion**" (my emphasis). It seems to me that we now have had a generation of politicians who have abandoned any attempt to go out and persuade the general public about anything!

Would the outcome of the attempted budget repair have been as dismal if Abbott and his ministers were out there in the public domain from Day 1 on, explaining – day-in, day-out – why these measures were necessary, why a moderate tightening of the belts was required? I doubt that very much. Indeed I believe the Government's capacity to negotiate their measures with a recalcitrant Senate would have been considerably stronger had they already convinced the general public of the need for these measures. They did not.

Regrettably that was not Abbott's only major leadership failure. The other one that stands out is his decision to abandon pursuing changes to Section 18C of the Racial Discrimination Act. In an environment in which we are witnessing an ever increasing encroachment on all of our freedoms Abbott's chickening out of the freedom of speech issue was an utter disgrace. I will have more to say on the issue of freedom more generally elsewhere in this book. Here I will only add the following. The way Abbott dealt with the 18C issue is symptomatic of the general malaise of conservatism in the West. Contemporary conservatives often have no clear idea what their core values are, and even when they do, they are not brave enough to stand up for them.

Then came 2019 and another "unwinnable" election. We now know how ScoMo prevailed against all odds and contrary to most political commentators' expectations. I will confess that Scott Morrison was a bit of an enigma for me at first. I think I have subsequently come to understand him a bit better.

"The PM is the embodiment of middle-ground pragmatism," proclaims veteran political commentator Paul Kelly in *The Australian* (3 February 2021). I beg to differ. ScoMo is the embodiment of political opportunism, in my humble view. This came into full view at the time of the 2018 Liberal party leadership crisis. Morrison played the faithful deputy to perfection until one minute to midnight, then at the perfect moment he came out of literally nowhere and stole the party's leadership from Peter Dutton – the man who had done the hard work causing the spill and challenging Turnbull. It was a spectacular political feat.

I do not wish to be unduly unfair to Morrison. He has an exceptionally sharp mind, and is across not only his own brief, but practically across every major ministerial portfolio's brief – like no other politician I have seen. ScoMo's loyalty to his family and his unreserved adoration of his wife and his daughters are admirable, indeed heart-warming. And as a political operative, he is highly disciplined, focused, committed and extremely hard-working. The way Morrison carried the whole 2019 election campaign on his shoulders was unbelievable. He almost single-handedly won the election for his party. I don't believe that even his worst enemies failed to be impressed.

And then suddenly all horizons opened up for him politically. The principal powerbrokers who had sown division in the Liberal party for more than 10 years were out of the parliament and out of the way. Not a single political figure inside the parliamentary party was presenting a threat to him – then or in the foreseeable future. The party room was more united than it had been in living memory. Indeed, thanks in large part to ScoMo's stunning victory, the PM had acquired absolute authority over his parliamentary colleagues and was in complete control of the party. And on the other side of the fence you had a Labor opposition which was utterly demoralised after losing the "unlosable" election, a party in organisational chaos and with no clear policy direction.

At this point in time the sky was the limit for a conviction leader in ScoMo's position. Few would have been the things that he would have failed to achieve had he had the vision and the determination to pursue them. To say nothing of the leadership opportunities arising from a major crisis like the COVID pandemic – opportunities to reshape the economy, to initiate sorely needed Industrial Relations reform, to change direction in energy policy, to start making Australia more self-sufficient and more resilient. That he almost completely failed to provide such leadership has been extremely disappointing. ScoMo has emerged as perhaps the most risk-averse political figure in contemporary Australia and, given the general risk-averseness of the current crop of politicians, this is a very high bar to pass. I think his recent conversion to the climate change orthodoxy has come as a bitter disappointment to the more conservatively leaning Liberal supporters. There is evidence that many of them feel politically orphaned, left without a political party representing them. I doubt that many of them will be keen to vote Liberal at the 2022 election and will switch to the

Liberal Democrats or One Nation.

I almost despair when I think of the average politician these days. Based on what they say, based on the positions they take, based on the policies they support, it seems to me that the vast majority of them lack political and even moral courage. My impression is that most contemporary politicians are driven by either political expediency or ideological bias (or both) and because of that they tend to embrace fashionable causes which often are not only not aligned with the interests of ordinary Australians, but in many cases can have destructive social, cultural and economic consequences. The most glaring example is climate change. This is not the place or time to engage in a lengthy polemic on the merits (or lack thereof) of the global warming orthodoxy. The fact that in around 40 years the so called climate science has failed to produce any remotely accurate predictions of how the earth's climate will evolve should give even the "true believers" a bit of a pause. Rising seas, sinking islands, melting glaciers, vanishing polar bears, more and more devastating cyclones – which of these has materialised? To say nothing of the fact that in the last 20 odd years global temperatures have barely nudged upwards, even though we have continued to pump larger and larger amounts of carbon dioxide in the atmosphere.

As you know, if the data does not align well with the theory, you can't really blame the data.

To ignore this reality and to continue to pursue climate policies which have no effect on the climate whatsoever while hurting ordinary people is not just unreasonable – it is weak and cowardly. Yet the vast majority of politicians continue to support, vocally or silently, these policies. And this happens when (according to media commentators) a sizable number of them, both Labor and Coalition, have privately confessed that they are sceptical about the climate orthodoxy.

By their attitudes to the climate controversy alone, most politicians can roughly be divided into three categories: complete hypocrites, unimaginably dumb or ideologically blinded (and I admit that the practical difference between the latter two is negligible). Tony Abbott was famously overheard a few years ago to describe global warming as "complete crap". Whether this is a fair description of the climate change science is debatable, although a bit of healthy scepticism is thoroughly justified. Abbot, however, later on buckled to admittedly relentless pressure from the left-wing media and walked away from his statement. It is highly doubtful that someone with his strong conservative views actually changed his mind about that and, if this assessment is correct, it means that he behaved like a hypocrite (and coward). On the background of all this, the small number of major party politicians who have been courageous enough to stand up (at their peril) against the climate orthodoxy – the (ex-) Liberal Craig Kelly and a handful of Nationals come to mind – fully deserve our respect and admiration.

I am not even remotely tempted to delve into state-level politics. The level of mediocrity that reigns among our state politicians, with very few exceptions, is staggering and immensely depressing.

There seems to be an obsession among contemporary politicians to be perceived as "nice people", with most of their actions and behaviours solely geared to generate such a perception among the voting public. They are not here to provide leadership, to conduct economic reform, to address the serious challenges the country has to deal with. They are here to be nice.

In Season 1 of the highly popular TV show *House* a patient peeved by the abrasiveness of House's behaviour asks another doctor: "Is he (House) a good man?" "He is a good doctor," replies the other medic. "Can you be a good doctor without being a good man?" asks the patient. The answer is undeniably Yes. Being a highly competent professional is by no way predicated on being a nice human being. Can you be a good leader without being a good person? Absolutely. Former US President Trump is a glaring example. I find him truly appalling as a human being – a shallow, rude, uncultured, hugely narcissistic person. Yet an objective assessment of his presidency would show that, alongside a few notable failures, he did provide strong leadership – particularly in relation to the economy, but also elsewhere, including standing up to China, genuine attempts (but not entirely successful) to extract America from the multiple military quagmires that previous administrations plunged it in, and making more progress towards peace in the Middle East than any other president in living memory. If the conversation is about actual achievements, Trump was immeasurably more successful than many previous presidents, especially Obama whose greatest (and perhaps only) virtue was his public speaking skills. It would be very hard to deny that, at least until the pandemic, America thrived economically under Trump's leadership, with strong growth and virtually no unemployment.

In a recent interview on the popular *Triggernometry* podcast, Nick Buckley[1] said: "If you are trained to be a leader in any field, if you are trained to improve the lives of people you care about, then you need to do what's right, not what's convenient."

Lack of leadership is, more than anything else, Australia's politicians' worst crime. They deliberately put themselves out

---

1   According to Wikipedia, Nick Buckley (from Manchester, England) was appointed to the Order of the British Empire in December 2019. He spent 15 years working with the homeless. In 2011, he founded Mancunian Way, a charity which fired him in 2020 for criticising BLM.

there, they spare no effort to get themselves into a leadership position. Then they unabashedly indulge the perks and privileges of power, but fail to provide leadership. This is disgraceful, it is an act of betrayal.

Failure of leadership can be observed across most of the Government's portfolios. I will briefly discuss two: immigration and education.

I am very strongly pro immigration. For a sparsely populated country like Australia, immigration can be of enormous benefit. It is undeniable that historically immigrants have contributed immensely and have been an integral part of Australia's success story. But in the last two or three decades Australia's Governments have used mass immigration as a blunt economic instrument. Artificially strong population growth increases demand for goods and services and boosts the economy. But for how long can you continue adding over a quarter of a million people per annum – almost exclusively to the populations of the two largest cities? No one (of political consequence) seems to give a thought to the people of Western Sydney (and the respective suburbs of Melbourne) and the negative impact that overpopulation has had on their quality of life. No one bothers to consider the complexities and the scope of the problems associated with integrating – socially, culturally and economically – such gigantic influxes of new residents.

I recently finished reading Douglas Murray's book *The Strange Death of Europe*. It was one of the most depressing books I had read for as far back as I can remember. The way immigration in Europe (and to a lesser extent, here in Australia) has been handled for several decades, but especially since the beginning of the century is a clear example of politicians' inability – and not infrequently blatant denial – to recognise the risks of very high levels of immigration and the destructive consequences it can have. It should not require a profound insight to realise that bringing in very large numbers of people from completely different cultural backgrounds will inevitably have very disruptive effects on the social and cultural fabric of the host community. What I find particularly disturbing is that most political leaders continue to deny the problem in the face of glaring facts, in the face of compelling evidence of this social disruption happening all over Western Europe. All you need to do is go and visit some of the notorious suburbs of Paris, Stockholm and even Brussels to see the monster that uncontrolled mass immigration has created. These are essentially ethnic enclaves where the local majority speak a language different from the language of the mainstream community and where life is lived in accordance with the social, cultural and religious norms of the enclave's majority – irrespective of how much these norms may be incompatible with the social, cultural and religious norms of the mainstream community. How can you have a unified nation with a number of insulated mini-nations inside it?

Regrettably, after two decades of uncontrolled immigration, very much the same – albeit to a lesser extent, so far – is already happening in Australia. While I have not myself been out there in an anthropological exploration of the metropolitan suburbs, I can provide a telling example from my personal experience. As part of my job at the University of Newcastle I have been involved in supervising numerous doctoral candidates – almost all of them international students, typically from Asia and the Middle East. This was the case of a relatively recent PhD student from Saudi Arabia. Not long after he arrived in Australia to commence his degree I received an email from him inquiring whether it would be OK to do his program by distance, from Sydney. I said *No, Newcastle University does not offer research programs by distance*. And then I went on to amplify the benefits of Newcastle as a place of residence – a lovely city that offers a great lifestyle at perhaps half of the living costs of Sydney. You see, I made the assumption that one often makes when someone chooses Sydney over places like Newcastle and Wollongong. I assumed he chose Sydney because of its presumed urban, cultural, tourist, etc., attractions rather than "slumming" it in the "boring provinces". I assumed wrongly. He chose Sydney because, in his own words, *in Lakemba I feel like I am at home, in Saudi Arabia*!

I will leave aside the question why some migrants come to Australia when they wish to live their lives strictly according to the norms and values of their country of origin. I just say – if that is the lifestyle that suits you, stay where you are.

Controlled immigration, on the other hand, can be of immense value. Take the Skilled stream in Australia. It is designed to bring in migrants who are young, healthy, very highly educated, often with at least some professional experience. Most of them are strongly motivated to work and succeed in their field, and are characterised by a high work ethic.

Humans are perhaps the most expensive resource. In most circumstances it takes well over two decades from a child's birth to the time they have completed their tertiary education and have commenced their professional career. It may not be easy to put a cost to this, but I wouldn't be surprised if raising a child in contemporary Australia up to and beyond their university degree would cost up to one million dollars (or even more). Getting migrants through the Skilled stream provides Australia with high-quality human resources for free. It's a win-win – the newcomers gain from living in this wonderful country and Australia gains from their professional skills and hard work.

But there is another angle to the immigration issue which many are unaware of or have chosen to ignore. Through the Skilled stream, Australia brings in a highly motivated work force at a time when an increasing number of ethnic Australians (more often than not – Anglo-Australians) choose not to work, choose to live on the dole.

I have worked as an educator for over 35 years already. I know that the benefits of good education cannot be overstated. Education is perhaps the strongest determinant of success later in life. Better educated people live on average more prosperous and successful lives. Good education is an immense advantage – not only for the individual who has it, but also for the community generally, because the community as a whole gains from the expertise of its highly educated members.

When I first arrived in this country, I took an almost contemptuous view of Australia's public school education. Whenever I looked into a classroom I could detect no order or structure to what was taking place there. And also in terms of declarative knowledge specifically, the Aussie school kids seemed to be lagging behind by at least a year by comparison with their Bulgarian counterparts. I don't know how many times I have heard recently arrived Bulgarian kids say – *what they are now teaching us in class, we learned in Bulgaria two years ago.*

But with the passage of time and some further reflection, I started to revise my earlier impressions. So what if what took place in the classroom seemed lax and unstructured? So what if the Aussie kids learned some conceptual stuff a bit later than in other parts of the world? The only thing that counts is results. Quite obviously the type of public school education that the Aussies were getting had suited them well enough. Would Australia have become one of the most prosperous and successful countries in the world if her education system and standards were a failure?

I also came across some data from PISA assessments (Programme of International Student Assessment) which ranked Aussie school kids among the best in the world based on their performance in reading, maths and science. How much more evidence do you need to accept that Australian public school education works well enough?

Or should I have said "worked"? Because what was the case 20 years or so ago is no longer the case. "Australia has plunged in global education rankings," announced *The Australian* on 4 December 2019. "Plunged" may be a disagreeable term to some, but is not way off the mark. In the 2003 PISA global assessments, 15-year-old Australian school kids came fourth in reading. They were 16th in 2018; comparable slumps in ranking were recorded in maths and science. This downward trend in academic achievement has occurred despite the fact that during the same period government funding for school education grew very substantially.

Again according to *The Australian* newspaper, "Australian students are now more than 3½ years behind their Chinese peers." It is notable that Chinese school students have been able to significantly outperform their Aussie "colleagues" at a fraction of the funding and with classes that are often three times the average size of an Australian class.

Our pollies' approach to education is symptomatic of the way their minds operate. If a problem is identified, throw money at it. If that doesn't help, throw more money at it. But a simple comparison with China quite clearly shows that it has not been lack of sufficient funding that is at the root of the decline in Australian school kids' academic achievement we have witnessed over the past two decades.

If it is not the funding, what then is the problem underlying Aussie school kids' underachievement? This is a huge question requiring a much more extensive analysis and discussion than this book could offer, but I will give it a brief go here.

Regrettably education has not been immune to the destructive cultural trends I have described elsewhere in this book. We have seen both the school curriculum and the teaching methodology contaminated by fashionable lefty ideas – often completely devoid of any evidential basis for their capacity to produce viable results. We have seen the introduction of large scale programs (such as *Safe Schools*) essentially designed to indoctrinate our children into fashionable social justice causes, which not only do not contribute to the development of academic competence, but actually deter from it. Classroom time devoted to teaching and learning is a finite resource. When you spend valuable class time instructing critical race theory to adolescents, there will not be enough time to teach them how to read and write, or to multiply. When you ignore centuries of solid evidence of the efficacy of direct instruction and experiment with fancy (but unproven) new teaching methods and techniques, education standards unavoidably decline.

Indeed, you do not need to go back centuries to find compelling evidence of what works and works extremely well. Just take a look at what has been happening at the *Michaela Community School* in Wembley, Northwest London. It is an independent school which operates on two fundamental principles: direct instruction and uncompromising discipline. Admission into the School is premised on applicants (and their parents) accepting to behave in full compliance with the School's rules and regulations. Upon entering the School in the morning, *Michaela*'s students are required to submit their phones and other mobile devices to the teachers and can retrieve them at the end of the school day. No running and/or screaming takes place in the School's corridors, let alone inside the classroom. The teachers are in complete control of their classrooms. Their teaching involves explicit direct instruction.

That this educational model works very well – indeed, is stunningly successful – was demonstrated in the most compelling fashion when in 2019 this School's students performed twice as well as the UK average on the General Certificate of Secondary Education (roughly – the British version of the High School Certificate), despite the fact that the majority of the kids are from disadvantaged backgrounds. It is also noteworthy that the School's conditions, in particular the uncompromising discipline, are not at the expense of the children's mental and/or emotional wellbeing. Quite the opposite is the case. Most children not only report that they are happy, but also that they adore the School and the teachers. Demand for admission into the *Michaela Community School* by far exceeds its capacity.

No one will deny that teachers and curriculum and teaching methodology all matter. What the case of the *Michaela Community School* also shows us is the immense importance of discipline. But why should that come as a surprise to anyone? It should be glaringly obvious that where chaos reigns, cognition dwindles. In order for teachers to be able to teach (and for children to learn), teachers need to have an orderly and structured classroom environment.

However, the term 'discipline' seems in recent years to have become a dirty word in the context of Australian public school education. During the same period when we saw a slump in the academic performance of Australian school children we have also seen badly deteriorating classroom discipline in Australian public schools. "Australia ranked a lowly 70th out of 77 participating nations in the OECD's 2018 index of disciplinary climate," proclaims *The Sydney Morning Herald* on 4 December 2019. The sad reality is that Australian teachers are no longer in control of their classrooms.

Perhaps the worst aspect of the toxic new culture that has taken hold of our public schools is that it is a culture of appeasement. Cognitive excellence and academic achievement are no longer the objective. Everything which takes place in the classroom is geared towards making the children feel good about themselves, irrespective of how well or otherwise they perform academically. We are raising a generation of incompetent self-centred sooks – not well-adjusted, confident, high-achieving individuals.

I am staggered by the arrogance of ideologically driven politicians and bureaucrats who recklessly conduct large-scale experiments with our children's education imperilling the future of a whole generation.

To be fair to the pollies, we should not entirely exonerate the parents in relation to what has been happening with our school education. Where have the parents been all along? Why have so many of them remained blind to the inroads of the toxic new culture?

To be fair to the pollies more broadly, the Australian voters also deserve a bit of a drubbing. One of the wisdoms of veteran Labor politician (and more recently political commentator) Graham Richardson is that the voters always get it right. I like Richo a lot, but respectfully disagree. I think the voters do **eventually** hit the mark although it is not unheard of to shoot a few blanks before they get there. There is a curious pattern whereby voters tend to get into experimental mode at times when they are particularly well off. It is like wealth and wellbeing make them complacent and they say – why not give the other guy a go? And then when the other guy's reckless policies start really hurting them, only then do they come to their electoral senses.

The 2007 Federal Election comes to mind in that regard. Regardless of the unparalleled growth in prosperity that Australians experienced during the Howard years, they voted Rudd in and thus brought about the political chaos of the next 12 years. Why did the majority of the voters choose to reject what had undeniably been an exceptionally successful government and opt for something that they could not possibly be sure would work as well? I think that some voters did have genuine and legitimate reasons to dislike the Howard Government and to want to replace it – the Iraq war comes to mind, among other things. But it seems to me that after a decade the majority of the voting public had simply gotten tired of John Howard and wanted a fresh face. I suspect that many of them experienced voter regret not too long thereafter.

There is an old saying according to which every man deserves his wife and every nation deserves its government. I don't dare to embark on the treacherous territory of gender relations and will withhold any commentary on the former, but it is undeniable that the governments we get are the governments we, the people, (s)elect, therefore we fully deserve them. I am sick of hearing commentators bemoan the terrible fate of Victorians under Dan Andrews' handling of the pandemic. Andrews is in the State's driver's seat solely because the Victorian public have repeatedly voted him in and, if current opinion polls are not completely off the mark, intend to vote him in again. Andrews is exactly what they deserve – nothing less, nothing more.

To end this chapter on a positive note, one can see the emergence of a new generation of politicians – almost exclusively on the right – like Amanda Stoker, James Patterson, Andrew Hastie (not a comprehensive list), who are not only very intelligent and articulate, but are prepared to stand up for their values. What a refreshing and reassuring change!

Not all is lost on the political front in Australia.

5

The Indigenous Australians

This was in many respects the most difficult chapter to write. It deals with an extraordinarily complex and sensitive issue; an issue with often competing social, cultural and ethical dimensions; an issue with sometimes rather disturbing, even confronting, manifestations; an issue that many people prefer not to talk about.

Let me preface this narrative by reminding the reader that, prior to turning up on Australia's metaphorical shores, my knowledge of Australia was limited to what I read in a short one-paragraph entry in a world encyclopaedia; to the best of my memory, there was nothing in it about the Indigenous people. Yes, I vaguely knew of Australia's Aborigines. Somewhere in a literary work I had read about the boomerang – this ingenious hunting tool of the Aborigines which conveniently swoops back to the thrower saving them the time and effort to have to go and retrieve it. And that was literally all I knew. As I pointed out in the opening pages of this book, I came to this country with a completely open mind, unencumbered by prior bias or prejudice.

Chapter 2 details my first weeks and months in Australia, and the rather steep learning curve they involved of finding out about life in my new country and overcoming cultural differences.

But within a year or two I had managed to put together a fairly coherent picture of contemporary Australia. With one exception – the Indigenous question. I readily confess it took me quite a few years to even start getting my head around it.

It would be very hard, perhaps impossible, for people born and raised in this country to properly appreciate how confusing the Indigenous question can be to a newcomer, especially someone with little or no prior knowledge of Australian history. What this particular newcomer observed in the early years of his residence here were two incongruous trends. On the one hand I noticed something akin to an uneasy hushed silence among the majority of ordinary Australians on Indigenous issues, a very distinct reluctance to talk on this topic at all. And on the other hand we had a relatively small, but extremely vocal section of the media and the academe who ceaselessly decried Australia's brutally racist treatment of the country's Indigenous people.

Let me clarify that neither my personal, nor my professional circumstances have provided me with opportunities for extensive contacts with Australians of Indigenous heritage. Maybe this has in part been due to not having too many of them in the Newcastle/Hunter region. The relatively small number of Indigenous individuals that I have had a chance to interact with I found without exception to be gentle, quiet and very pleasant on a personal level. I have never been out on any of the remote settlements, although I have read a great deal about them in various public and media sources. I have also heard a fair bit about them from fellow linguists who spent time in one or more of them doing fieldwork.

A lot of the confusion in the earlier days stemmed from the fact that I was not witnessing anything even remotely supporting the ongoing rant about the racist treatment of the Indigenous people – I simply did not see any evidence of this alleged racism anywhere around me. Quite the opposite! Wherever I looked I could only see overwhelmingly positive attitudes to Australia's Indigenous people, huge amounts of good will and desire to help where help was needed.

At work I noticed how every formal occasion without exception (even humble departmental meetings) started with an acknowledgement of the Traditional Custodians.

In the earliest days and weeks when I was trying very hard to find a job, I noticed that practically all applications for government/public employment included a section labelled "equal opportunity" which was specifically for applicants of Indigenous heritage. When you read the small print you quickly realised that this was not about "equal opportunity" – this was a policy to select an Indigenous applicant whenever one was available. It was in effect preferential treatment, a form of positive discrimination.

As I commenced my lectureship at the University I almost immediately noticed how strongly studies of Indigenous history/culture/languages were promoted. With the passage of time I also became aware of attempts on the part of some academics to "game" the system by including an Indigenous "angle" to their research – anything to get hold of the much coveted research grant. (Try to get a promotion without a few of these under your academic belt!) More recently I became aware of not an insignificant number of individuals (often with a high social profile) taking on an Indigenous identity despite not having a trace of Indigenous heritage. Indeed, this seems to have become so wide-spread that has outraged some Indigenous leaders who have quite recently lodged a complaint with the NSW Independent Commission Against Corruption about the disproportionally large number of University of Sydney staff and students taking on an Indigenous identity. It seems to me that this alone dispels the myth of Indigenous oppression/discrimination. It is a strategy to gain benefits, not a desire to become a member of a "brutally oppressed" minority.

In 2005 the University of Newcastle underwent a substantial "restructuring", which was the code word for wide-ranging job cuts. About 20% of staff were made redundant across every department, with one exception – the Wollotuka Institute (the Department of Indigenous Studies).

I also learned about a number of Government and non-Government agencies whose sole purpose was to support Indigenous people in practically all aspects of their lives. And there was also the welfare spending that the Federal Government directs specifically to Indigenous issues – running in the tens of billions of dollars every year. According to a recent report by the Productivity Commission, at around $45,000 per annum the welfare expenditure per Indigenous person is more than twice the rate for non-Indigenous Australians.

In summary, nothing in what I could see around me pointed to the wide-spread mistreatment of Indigenous people loudly proclaimed by the political activists.

To avoid misunderstanding, I am not suggesting that Australia is completely free of racism or bigotry. Knowing what we know about the human condition, this would be an unsustainable position. Nice as most Australians are, they are not immune to human failings. There are idiots here, as there are elsewhere around the world. I have read credible historical accounts of incidents involving racist and discriminatory attitudes to Indigenous people. As I suggested earlier, I have not personally witnessed such attitudes in contemporary Australia. My impression is that the Aussies have gone a very long way towards eradicating such attitudes, and that today's Australia is as racism-free as any country can be (i.e., if it is not exclusively populated by saints) – certainly as racism-free as any place around the world.

Now I come to the more difficult part of this narrative – the part about the remote settlements. As the years rolled on, the wall of silence started to crack here and there, and gradually a picture of what life in some of these remote settlements was like started to emerge. The major breakthrough for me occurred in the mid-noughties when I chanced upon NT prosecutor Dr. Nanette Rogers' report on violence and abuse in remote settlements in the Northern Territory. About ten years later came the Smallbone report. Meanwhile I was becoming aware of a range of other facts in media publications and institutional reports, revealing stark differences – often by orders of magnitude – between the Indigenous people and the mainstream community in terms of life expectancy, health (especially chronic diseases, like diabetes), employment, education, incarceration and imprisonment, domestic violence, child neglect and child abuse (including child rape).

It is not the goal of this book to examine these facts in detail. They are out there for anyone to see them – that is, if they wish to see them. But these facts painted a rather dystopian picture of life in some of the remote settlements – typically small communities somewhere in the outback, hundreds of kilometres away from any other settlement, with next to no connection or communication with the rest of the country, with poor living conditions, virtually no employment opportunities, poor levels of education, inferior healthcare. At least to me it looked like these people were consigned to a life without purpose, without aspirations, without opportunities for personal growth, a life without meaning…

There can be no stronger indictment of the conditions in some of the remote settlements than the incidence of Indigenous teenage suicide occurring at a rate which is way above the national average. Isn't adolescence the time when young people overflow with life, with optimism, with grand designs for the future, a time when you feel invincible, immortal, when you can see no frontiers ahead that you cannot conquer? Can there be a greater tragedy than a 15-year-old deciding to take their own life? Can you imagine the overwhelming hopelessness and despair that can so take hold of a teenager's soul as to compel them to take this tragic step?

Extremely disturbing as this picture is, for me the more astonishing question was how this could possibly be allowed to happen in one of the most advanced and affluent countries in the world – a country which takes pride in being a fully functioning democracy.

In the left's narrative, this sorry state of affairs is ultimately the consequence of a historical event that took place two and a half centuries ago – the arrival of the British fleet and the white settlement that followed. In its essence, this is a claim that the "historical impacts of colonisation" were so severe and left such a profound "cross-generational trauma" on the Indigenous population, that they imperil the normal functioning of Indigenous individuals and communities even today.

I am not a historian and it is certainly not among the goals of this book to (re-)write Australia's history. But the book is in part about what I have learned about the history and the views that I have subsequently formed – views which I have promised to share fully and without holding back.

There has been a strong attempt on the part of the political activists to paint a highly romanticised picture of Indigenous life prior to colonisation – a tranquil and peaceful life in harmonious co-existence with the environment. And then the evil British colonisers came in and took all this away, or so the left's narrative goes.

You do not need to be a historian to know how unrealistic such a picture is. Anyone who has spent just a few years on this continent would know how harsh the Australian environment can be. This is the land of searing heats and flooding rains, of destructive storms and catastrophic fires, to say nothing of the abundance of deadly fauna (spiders, snakes, sharks, crocks, you name it). Imagine what life in these conditions would have been like – without the protection of our solid houses, without the amenities and conveniences of modernity, without the support of the specialised technology and highly trained personnel we have come to rely on so much. There is evidence that the Indigenous Australians had become remarkably skilled at managing various aspects of the environment, but regardless of that their lives cannot have been easy, let alone enjoyable. Life was a daily struggle for survival – nothing less, nothing more.

This is not to say that the arrival of the British fleet and the white settlement that followed were not traumatic to the local inhabitants. What occurred was extremely disruptive – it literally turned their world upside down, almost overnight. It caused them considerable suffering. Especially in the early days, Indigenous people were often abused, some were even murdered. Regrettably, there is nothing particularly unusual or surprising in what happened. Abuse and mistreatment of completely innocent people have unfortunately always been an integral part of wars, conflicts, colonisation. History abounds with examples, even very recent ones (remember Abu Ghraib).

"History, in short, is not a very nice place," as Joe Hildebrand wrote in a brilliant piece on this topic.

But is it fair to characterise the British settlement of Australia as **invasion** or **genocide**, as the activists gleefully do? I am not sure it is. It is true that some of the settlers committed acts of brutality and even murder to the local inhabitants, but there is no evidence to suggest that the new administration as a whole had hostile attitudes to the Indigenous people, let alone an intention to exterminate them. There is in fact solid evidence that the new administration took an essentially positive and constructive approach to the local inhabitants and the administration's intent was broadly to establish and maintain a positive and constructive relationship with them.

Indeed, when put in historical context, the British settlement of Australia was by a far margin not as brutal or ruthless as colonisation elsewhere around the world. For your reference, check what happened to the Indigenous peoples of Latin America when the Spanish started arriving there in the early 16th century. Check your facts about Belgian colonisation in Africa or Dutch colonisation in Asia (and elsewhere). By comparison, the British settlement of Australia was a pretty innocuous affair.

But regardless of how right or wrong my perceptions of the history are, I find it rather hard to give much credence to the attempt to explain current social problems by reference to historical events which occurred centuries ago. Remember, there is hardly a nation or an ethnic group anywhere on earth which has not experienced an adverse event at some point in its history – in many cases much more traumatic than what happened during Australia's colonisation. Do I get to claim "cross-generational trauma", because Bulgaria was under the brutal occupation of the Ottoman Empire for 500 years, until almost the end of the 19th century? Does the Middle East get to claim "cross-generational trauma" for the Crusades which took place in the early middle centuries?

The lack of validity of the "cross-generational trauma" argument aside, this narrative has contributed very little to resolving the very real and ongoing problems of Indigenous people in contemporary Australia. Quite the contrary – arguments like it have been instrumental in aggravating the situation in at least two ways. Playing the "cross-generational trauma" card in effect denies any agency to Indigenous people; it infantilises them and reduces them to a mob who lack the capacity to make their own decisions or even take care of themselves. Such condescending attitudes are on display in the extraordinary leniency with which some representatives of the judiciary treat Indigenous crime. I have read media reports that in some cases Indigenous perpetrators avoid a jail sentence even for very serious crimes, like rape and murder. The underlying message is – they do not know what they are doing, which is why we cannot punish them in the same way we would punish a non-Indigenous perpetrator. What we are seeing here is a very deliberate choice to treat some individuals differently **solely on the basis of these individuals' race/ethnicity**. But isn't that the dictionary definition of racism?

The "cross-generational trauma" narrative has also been responsible in fostering a strong sense of historical guilt among many of the ethnic Anglo-Australians. They are held responsible for what happened two and a half centuries ago and therefore they are responsible for the "cross-generational trauma" and the subsequent (and ongoing) plight of Australia's Indigenous people.

This historical guilt is profoundly illogical – it defies any common sense. I imagine it may be possible to trace a handful of the ethnic Anglo-Australians back to the original settlers. So what? How can you hold someone responsible for what a very distant ancestor did or didn't do centuries ago? It is utterly absurd. And let us also not forget that in today's Australia the ethnic Anglo-Australians are becoming an ever diminishing minority.

Nowadays well above half of the people living on this continent are first- and second-generation immigrants, the vast majority of them from non-English speaking backgrounds. I am proudly one of them. Let me say this very clearly – no one can hold us or our children responsible for the historical events of two and a half centuries ago in Australia. We had absolutely nothing to do with what happened then, not even by a by a remote (and completely irrelevant) ancestral connection.

The "cross-generational trauma" argument is not only deeply flawed and divisive, but is also counterproductive. It has done very little to improve the wellbeing of Australia's Indigenous people, while at the same time cowing many ordinary Australians and making them reluctant to actively address Indigenous issues – lest they are (again) accused of racism. The "cross-generational trauma" argument has largely been responsible for the "wall of silence" I experienced on arrival. Failure on the part of most ordinary Australians to actively engage in public discourse on Indigenous issues and to demand solutions from our political and community leaders has in effect led to further entrenching Indigenous disadvantage.

The cynic in me wonders whether the "cross-generational trauma" narrative is driven by a genuine desire to improve the lot of Indigenous people. If their situation radically improved, many activists will be left without a moral cause, and many bureaucrats will be left without a lucrative job. Very much like the priest in Richard Russo's brilliant novel *Nobody's Fool*, they seem "to understand that to wish people less wretched would be to put [themselves] out of a job."

There are certainly historical lessons to be learned from the time of the British settlement. Should we, however, all be ashamed? Should we all bear the guilt for what happened centuries ago?

Definitely not. It seems to me that there is immensely more to be ashamed of in contemporary Australia than what occurred 250 years ago. Besides, what happened then is history. We cannot control the past. There is not a single bit that we can do to change it. We do have control over the present. What is happening NOW with Australia's Indigenous people is an absolute disgrace. That we are allowing for this situation to go on is something that we all should be profoundly ashamed of.

If "cross-generational trauma" is not the reason for what is occurring in the remote settlements, then why do we have this situation? This is undeniably a complex and difficult question, one which many people in Australia would prefer not to ask. According to the great Jacinta Price (*The Australian*, 22 January 2020), Indigenous cultural traditions and customary law are at least in part responsible for the problems (like domestic violence and child neglect and abuse) that are so pervasive in the remote settlements. Knowing who Jacinta Price is and where she is coming from, it is impossible not to take such claims seriously. But while Indigenous culture/customs probably is an exacerbating factor, I am not sure at all it is the main driver of the misery that we see in some of the remote settlements. It seems to me that the whole setup of these settlements is the principal driver.

Imagine a small community which is geographically remote and essentially insulated, with few or no local businesses, with no industry, little or no meaningful employment; a community where there are few opportunities for participation in social and cultural events, such as sport or theatre or cinemas or restaurants; where alcohol and drug abuse is rampant; where there is little or no law enforcement. What do you think will happen? Would the picture be different if it were Caucasians or Asians or Middle-Easterners or Africans or any other race or ethnicity? I don't think so. It is not who these people are, it is the circumstances in which they live that cause the problems.

And now I gratefully switch to a much more positive note. Not all is bad with the Indigenous people in this country, not all of them lead hopeless and meaningless lives. Media celebrity and proud Indigenous man Stan Grant calls it "a quiet revolution." Grant's article (*The Australian*, 15 May 2020) describes a process of profound transformation, of remarkable growth in Indigenous personal and professional achievement and success, especially in the last 25 years or so. Grant presents a number of very impressive data to demonstrate this "quiet revolution": a 75% increase of the number of highly qualified Indigenous professionals, a more than doubling of the number of Indigenous university students, a near doubling of Indigenous individuals with postgraduate qualifications (among many others).

In Sam Grant's words, we are witnessing "the growth of a solidly middle-class Indigenous population", which he describes as "an extraordinary success". It undeniably is an extraordinary success which fully deserves to be celebrated, although many among the commentariat choose to ignore it. It is certainly notable that this success has occurred entirely outside of the remote settlements.

To me personally (after years of sometimes torturous reflection), these facts paint a picture of two strikingly different Indigenous stories. On the one hand we see the profound misery and hopelessness in many of the remote communities. On the other hand, we see remarkable Indigenous success and achievement – a growing number of Indigenous people leading meaningful and happy lives within the mainstream community.

Yes, I am mindful that the above is a broad generalisation, and that broad generalisations are by their nature also oversimplifications sweeping over many individual circumstances which do not all and always fully align with the generalisation. But that does not make it wrong.

Indeed, this generalisation could give us a model – a clear path forward. I think we have to provide every Indigenous person with the opportunities to experience the same success that Sam Grant tells us about, enable each and every one of them to become a medical professional, a teacher, a business entrepreneur, a tradie, an AFL star.

I am obviously not suggesting that anyone be forced to do anything they do not wish to do. I do not doubt that many Indigenous people will choose to continue living according to their traditional culture and customs. This is a choice that we should respect and fully support.

Comprehensive support for the remote settlements should remain as it is, but the Government should put in place a framework of powerful incentives for Indigenous people to move out and join the mainstream community if they choose to do so, especially the younger people. I am confident that there will be many among them who, given the right incentives, will embrace an opportunity to join the mainstream community, such as generous academic scholarships, promising jobs, better housing, etc.

But wouldn't that amount to integration (another dirty word in the left's lexicon)? And what about the Indigenous culture? Wouldn't that be at the expense of Indigenous culture?

There is not a shred of doubt in my mind that culture is very important. Besides, as a professional linguist and someone who has been a language enthusiast for close to half a century, I can appreciate better than most people the immensely important roles that language plays in practically all aspects of our lives. And from a purely linguistic point of view, Australia's Indigenous languages are absolutely fascinating as they possess a number of very unusual, perhaps even unique, structural and grammatical properties.

With all that said, it is unclear to me whether contemporary Indigenous culture is quite the same as Indigenous culture prior to white settlement. It has been inevitably contaminated by the dominant Western culture and is gradually being eroded.

Almost all of the Indigenous languages regrettably are on the verge of extinction. In many cases, there are few or no living native speakers of these languages. Unfortunately, language is not something that can be kept alive artificially. If a language has no speakers, it is a dead language. On the positive side, over the past few decades there has been a quite impressive research effort mostly by Australian linguists to examine and document as many of these languages as possible. These languages will not go into oblivion the way many other of the world's languages have historically.

Ultimately the question that we need to ask ourselves is – Is culture more important than human happiness? Is the life and wellbeing of children less important than culture? As far as I am concerned, the answer is unequivocally No.

How confident am I that something akin to what I am suggesting here can happen? I openly admit that I do not feel particularly optimistic in that regard. It is a diabolically complex and difficult reform, one which will take at least several decades to accomplish. Knowing what our political class is like, knowing how focused they are on short-termism, political expediency and their own political survival, it seems to me that the chances of this happening are virtually zero. Unless, of course, we – the ordinary

Australians – break the wall of silence and put some pressure on them. Because the pollies do respond to pressure. Australia's Indigenous people fully deserve this!

Interlude 3: On Freedom

A major leitmotif in the ideological narratives of the contemporary left (particularly in the English speaking democracies) concerns the alleged evilness of Western Civilization. Western Civilization is deeply sinful, racist (and white supremacist), misogynist, homophobic, bigoted, oppressive – you name it. In their extreme, such attitudes in effect refuse to associate any positive values with Western Civilization. This is, in my mind at least, yet another manifestation of a relatively recent phenomenon – a willful abandonment of reason and commonsense, complete detachment from reality, complete disregard for established facts and truths.

This is not to say that Western Civilization is entirely free of sin. There were brutal wars, oppression, racism, slavery, cruelty, all of that – in the West as in every other part of the world. Sin is embedded in the human condition and will be a part of humanity for as long as we survive as a species. But no fair-minded person can look at the facts, historically and currently, and fail to recognise that Western Civilization has also been incredibly successful in almost every conceivable way. Think of literature, (classical) music, visual art, film, architecture, etc., and the extraordinary number of unparalleled masterpieces that have been created over several centuries. Think of the unimaginable advances in science and technology. Think of the immense prosperity that Western Civilization has generated for most of its citizens, the massive growth of living standards. Western Civilization has given us, the ordinary people, a quality of life which has absolutely no historical parallels.

And think also of the vastly superior moral and ethical norms that we now live by thanks to Western Civilization. Think of the unparalleled human rights that people in the West enjoy. Think of our freedom. You do not have to be a historian to know there has never been a time in humanity's history when the ordinary individual was so free and so empowered, when ordinary people had the capacity to manage their own lives, to pursue their personal dreams, to build their happiness.

Tracing the origins of the West's success would be a fascinating academic journey. I believe that individual freedom has been a critical part of that success.

Freedom of speech is often presented as the most important freedom – a foundational human right without which a liberal democracy cannot function properly. Sociologist Frank Furedi disagrees arguing that freedom of conscience is even more important. While I do not have an argument with either of these views, it seems to me that it is unnecessary, perhaps even wrong, to qualify the term 'freedom' or to narrow it down to a particular type. It seems to me that it should be just *freedom*, full stop.

Individual freedom is the ultimate value – perhaps the most precious moral and intellectual resource that we possess. But it is not a God-given right. Many among those who have lived all of their lives in a liberal democracy do not seem to appreciate the fact that even by today's standards freedom is by far not a universal aspect of life everywhere around the world. Yes, one can find a relatively high degree of freedom in Europe and North America, in Australia and New Zealand, in Japan and South Korea, in Israel, India and Indonesia. There is certainly less freedom to be found in most of Latin America, and one would struggle to detect even remote elements of freedom elsewhere around the world. Think Russia, China, North Korea, Iran, Saudi Arabia – freedom is essentially a foreign concept in these places. My point is that even in the 21st century freedom is not as wide-spread and established around the world as some people in the West might be tempted to think. And in historical terms, freedom of the ordinary individual is a relatively recent phenomenon, probably going not much further back than a couple of centuries.

Many people fail to appreciate that most of the achievements of Western civilization over the past two or three centuries – industrial, technological, cultural – are very closely tied to the rise of individual freedom. Freedom empowered the ordinary person and unleashed an unprecedented surge of inventiveness, creativity and artistic talent. Would the four working-class boys from Liverpool have evolved as The Beatles in an unfree society, would we have had The Rolling Stones and Led Zeppelin? Would we have had college dropouts launching an IT revolution from their garages and creating a technological future that even the wildest imagination could not have conceived?

Most people living in a liberal democracy do not have a true appreciation of freedom. I am not passing judgements here. The things that we have always had we tend to take for granted. This is a very normal feature of the human psyche. Often we can only appreciate the value of something that we don't have or after we have lost it. People who do not have freedom or only have it to a limited degree value it much more than those who have enjoyed freedom throughout their lives. Having lived approximately half of my life in communism as an unfree person, I believe that I have a much greater appreciation of freedom than most of the people living nowadays in the West.

I am not an exception in that regard. Immigrants more generally have a greater appreciation of the West's achievements and of the substantial advantages of life in a Western democracy. In a recent *Triggernometry* interview Gad Staad articulated this very eloquently; he said:

> Some of the staunchest defenders of the Western tradition are immigrants, precisely because they have sampled from the wide buffet of possible societies. And they know that the miracle of the Western tradition is exactly that – it's a miracle, it's an anomaly. The history of humanity is not littered with free societies, individual dignity. That's not the default structure of the human condition. So it takes people who have existed in the default societies that are not congruent with the Western tradition to then come to the West, see the traditions that we have and say, *What the hell are you, morons, doing*? [...] If you've seen Venezuela, if you've seen the former Soviet Union, if you've seen Lebanon, then you know how beautiful Canada or the UK or the US historically have been and you want to fight for those values.

Attitudes to freedom differ among members of the same community, and also between different communities. After the collapse of the Soviet Bloc in Europe the former satellites of the Soviet Union started a difficult transition toward a more liberal-democratic social order. In Bulgaria, the first free parliamentary elections in half a century took place in June 1990. It was an unbelievably optimistic and uplifting period, overflowing with hope and positive expectations. These were crushed to the ground when the former communist party won an absolute majority in parliament! In the wake of the elections, for days and weeks I felt sick. I struggled to comprehend how it was possible for the slaves to freely elect their masters, their oppressors, their abusers. I came to the rather unsavoury conclusion that many Bulgarians did not like freedom. How else could one explain the 1990 election result?

In subsequent years I have come to realise that the Bulgarians are not unique in that regard, and that people who do not like freedom are represented in every community around the globe. These are the people who vote for the welfare state, for all kinds of bans and prohibitions, for creating all kinds of institutions and bureaucracies whose sole purpose is to absolve the citizens of personal responsibility.

An individual's attitude to freedom as a core value is a powerful determinant of this individual's world view more generally. You cannot value freedom and safety at the same time. Once you elevate the importance of safety as a value you unavoidably relinquish your freedom. (Should we be worried that safety has become an obsession in this country and elsewhere in the West?) You cannot value freedom and refuse to take responsibility for your own affairs. You abrogate your freedom when you delegate decision-making to someone else. Freedom lovers are control freaks – they want to take control of every aspect of their social and physical environment, because when their social and physical environments control them it is at the expense of their freedom.

In a recent conversation with a colleague I reminisced about my early adulthood in communist Bulgaria. I recalled this as the most care-free period of my life. It may sound absurd, but it was nevertheless unquestionably true. I was care-free in exactly the same way the marionettes are care-free in John Gray's political philosophy. I was care-free in the same way as prison inmates are – with a daily routine completely structured from dawn to dusk, utterly devoid of the responsibilities associated with agency and decision making.

Because individual freedom is also a burden. It is the burden of making decisions for yourself and for your family, and bearing the consequences of these decisions. Remember *The Shawshank*

Redemption, this 1994 masterpiece featuring Morgan Freeman and Tim Robbins. The film is a celebration of the irrepressible desire for freedom. Alas, it also shows how after years in the care-free world of jail freedom can become too much of a burden for some, it can become so overwhelming that a former inmate takes his own life.

Is this what is happening in today's Western world? People abandoning freedom, because it is too much of a burden?

Indeed, over the past several decades we have witnessed a disturbing process of an ever growing erosion of individual freedom. Contemporary Western societies are now a lot less free than they were 20 or 30 years ago. We have seen an unrelenting trend to impose more and more boundaries and restrictions on how people live their lives, on people's capacity to make their own decisions, to manage their own affairs – all presumably done in the name of our wellbeing.

There is also a strong parallel trend of absolving people of personal responsibility. This trend is particularly obvious in the judicial system where even very serious crimes (including violent ones) are often treated with astonishing leniency.

When people are denied the agency to make their own decisions and when the responsibility for the decisions they make is taken away from them, they cease being a free agent.

Many of us do not seem to realise that the essential purpose of a tremendous amount of the rules and regulations that governments nowadays impose (or should I say – inflict) on us is not so much to make our lives easier, but to make life easier for the Government. Take the arguably trivial example of the council regulation that all dogs must be on leash at all times, otherwise hefty fines apply.

The rationale is presumably to protect the general public from dogs whose owners are unable to control them. And there are undeniably a quite few of these – individuals who are too stupid or too irresponsible or too lazy to invest the necessary time and effort for training their pet dogs properly. The leash regulation is specifically for them, but it punishes everyone, including those of us who have done the right thing.

And there is another aspect to the leash "rule" which has attracted surprisingly little public attention, especially given how sensitive the community has become to any perceived instances of cruelty to animals. Keeping your poor puppy permanently constrained by their neck is punishing to them, it is in its essence a form of cruelty. But the council does not care for you or for your puppy. The council is quite happy to put in place a blanket regulation that denies everyone the freedom to manage their pet in whatever way they choose. The alternative is to only pursue and penalise dog owners who abuse this freedom. And that would require a considerably greater effort. Therein is the whole point of this exercise – to make the job of the councilors easier at your (and your pet's) expense. And we see the same exercise perpetuated at a large scale by all levels of government.

One rather controversial freedom which in Australia has over the decades been subject to more and more draconian restrictions concerns gun ownership. The prevailing "wisdom" is that the availability of guns in the community is bad, because it is associated with violent crime, especially murder. Look at what has been happening in America, with all those awful mass shootings. On the face of it, this is a position which is very hard to argue against. If there are no guns whatsoever, no one will be killed by a gun. But the picture is somewhat more nuanced than that.

Gun ownership is essentially an issue of personal freedom. Gun-related crime was conspicuously absent in communist Bulgaria (and generally elsewhere in totalitarian regimes). No one owned a firearm outside of the law enforcement apparatus. But individual freedom was as conspicuously missing from the scene.

Freedom more than anything else means personal responsibility – it falls on you to protect yourself, your family and your home. The government cannot guarantee your protection. This is an undeniable fact. I am not herewith implying any criticism of the Australian police for whom I have the highest admiration. I believe they do a stellar job in often very challenging circumstances. But it is impossible for the law-enforcement professionals to provide protection to everyone 24/7 – they simply can't be everywhere all of the time. Yes, they do their very best to respond to emergencies and to turn up at the location where they are needed, but it takes time – 10, 15, 20 minutes – which can sometimes be the difference between life and death.

A few years ago I experienced a rather disturbing incident. My daughter Ellena (in her early teens) and I had just returned home from a social event. It was almost midnight and we were putting together a very late supper, when we heard noises outside and became aware of objects being thrown at our windows. It looked like a bunch of perhaps half a dozen teenagers, either inebriated or high on something else, who were throwing raw eggs at the house. I tried to shout them away, told them I will call the police, but that did not make an impression and they continued circling around in a very menacing fashion. I felt extremely exposed and vulnerable, particularly scared for my young daughter's safety. Of course I did call 000 and asked for help. It probably took no more than 15 minutes for a police car to arrive (although it seemed like an eternity). An awful lot could have happened meanwhile. Luckily it didn't, but if it had happened, I would have been in no position to protect myself or, more importantly, my child. A parent's worst nightmare. The memory of it haunted me for a very long time.

To wrap up this unfortunate story, the young gang disappeared shortly before the police car turned up – they probably had someone on watch to give them the heads-up. The police officer was extremely courteous and helpful, the ultimate professional. He reassured us that we would not be bothered by the young rascals again. I am ashamed to say that it did not occur to me to ask the officer for his name – I was too distraught. But I remain eternally grateful to him.

My point is that even at the best of circumstances critical help cannot be provided exactly when we need it. Then why is the Government denying us the ability to protect ourselves – if we can and wish to do so? An incident from a few years ago (which I found particularly distressing to read about) provides a compelling illustration of this:

> A farmer who confronted a knife-wielding intruder, possibly affected by ice, entering his family home with a rifle has had his guns confiscated by police.
>
> David Dunstan used an unloaded rifle to stop the man entering his home as his three children lay sleeping inside.
>
> He claims he's being punished for protecting his family.

This also illustrates another extremely troubling cultural shift in Australia (and in the West generally). Nowadays we seem much more concerned for the finer feelings of the perpetrators than the wellbeing and safety of the victims.

And yet another very troubling cultural shift – pure emotion, rather than careful and thoughtful consideration of the facts, has become the ultimate (and often only) determinant in decision making about serious issues that affect us. Hundreds of lives are lost annually in Australia to traffic accidents. If the same number of lives were lost to gun violence, there would be an outrage. It doesn't even occur to anyone to propose a ban on all traffic, even though this would reduce traffic-related death to zero overnight. Tragic as all loss of life is, we accept that this is a price we pay for modernity – indeed, for the freedom of movement that motor vehicles afford us – and instead take common-sense measures to reduce this death toll. The vast majority of drivers are sensible and responsible, and we specifically target the ones who cause trouble.

There is plenty of evidence that the vast majority of gun owners are sensible and responsible. There is no conceivable reason to punish them or to deny them the right to protect themselves. Gun-related violence is almost exclusively perpetrated by criminals using illegal firearms. There is evidence from the USA that districts which are subject to strict gun-control restrictions are much more prone to violent crime than areas where gun ownership is freer. Which should not be entirely surprising. The prospect of being confronted by a resolute gun-toting home owner can have a dampening effect on the urge to commit a felony.

One could reasonably argue that the state of affairs with guns in America is extreme and that it is necessary to find a reasonable balance between gun freedoms and gun-related risks to the community. A sensible and considerate discussion is always welcome, with one important proviso – once a freedom starts to be eroded, this almost unavoidably leads to its complete loss.

A brief personal clarification to avoid misunderstanding – I have never owned a gun and do not have a particular desire to have one.

Individual freedom promotes creativity, imagination, self-expression. It enables people to do a tremendous amount of good. The erosion of personal freedoms, the ever increasing number of rules, regulations and restrictions, the relentless growth of government power (at all levels) strangles creativity and innovation. Did you know that innovation has almost completely disappeared in the West? That was what Matt Ridley claimed in an interview with Brendan O'Neill about Ridley's new book *How Innovation Works*. Innovation cannot thrive in a society shackled by infinite bans and regulations.

Innovation will not be the only victim of the loss of freedom. Once freedom completely disappears (and we seem to be unswervingly headed in that direction) the whole liberal democratic order will cease to exist, at least in the way we know it. The disturbing trends I have been mapping here came to a climax of sorts during the pandemic when we saw Governments assume extraordinary powers and strip the public of even the most basic rights and freedoms. Even more disturbingly, the public accepted this abuse of power (almost) without any resistance. Most seemed comfortable to give up their freedom and to allow the Government to control practically every aspect of their lives. Like sheep in search of a shepherd (see below)…

As I described in the first chapter of this book, I was an active and very enthusiastic participant in the democratisation processes taking in place in Bulgaria in the early 1990s. These processes gave rise to an explosion in public debate, often taking place in informal spaces, including on internet forums. I was a regular contributor to a now long extinct internet site called *Oshte Info* (= more info). This is where I read an essay on freedom penned by a guy called Bozhidar Marinov. It impressed me so much that I copied the piece and saved it on my computer. Below I have provided a slightly abridged translation of this essay. I think it makes a fitting end to this chapter.

Bozhidar Marinov in *Oshte Info*

29 March 2005

Slavery does not start with the slave owners. Slavery starts with the slaves. Slavery does not start with someone wielding a weapon and compelling people to work for them. It starts when people choose to relinquish looking after themselves and their families, and turn to someone else to provide the things they need. Slavery happens when people abandon the responsibility to make their own life decisions and delegate these decisions to someone else. The essence of slavery is in willfully opting for safety over freedom. Slavery constitutes the willful abdication of individual rights and responsibilities, and vesting other people or institutions with the discharge of these rights and responsibilities. Slavery is rooted in the sheep's instinct to find a shepherd – someone to take it out to pasture and to shear it.

In the contemporary world, slavery is the social welfare. It is in providing [free] health care to people who never take care of their own health. It is in providing retirement welfare to people who never devote a single thought to their own future. It is in providing free state education to the children of parents who happily procreate, but can't be bothered to take care of their offspring. Slavery is in imposing comprehensive regulations on how we live our lives and on the broader economy.

Slaves have no concept of a future and because of that can have no future. A nation of slaves has no future. In one way or another such a nation eventually perishes.

Only a free individual has a future. The future belongs to those who choose to take responsibility over it. Anything else is sheer delusion and empty utopia.*

* Marinov obviously had Bulgaria and the Bulgarians in mind when he wrote this piece. I think it applies more broadly.

6

The Media

I will again have to remind the reader that I spent the first 30-odd years of my life in communist Bulgaria where the media (radio, TV, newspapers) were totally controlled by the state and offered very little other than propaganda. For several decades there was just a single TV channel which, in addition to the local nonsense, allocated one day per week to broadcasting programs directly from the Soviet Union (on a Friday, all year round). If I remember correctly, this continued right up to the end of the 1970s. We had two national radio stations which complemented each other in terms of the propaganda that was delivered. There were a few different newspapers, but when I say "different" I mean they had different titles and sometimes different presentational formats, but in terms of content they were practically indistinguishable.

The collapse of communism in Eastern Europe in the late 1980s and the early 1990s brought about a welcome change in the media environment. We initially saw a strong rise of independent newspapers, followed by radio stations and TV channels. After decades of information vacuum, having access to a free press offering a broad range of information and a true diversity of views was a wonderfully liberating experience.

My first exposure to commercial TV in Australia involved watching an Alistair McClean action movie. I was completely unused to commercial breaks and therefore completely unprepared for them. When the first one occurred I had a blank moment or two. What was taking place on the screen did not make any sense. One moment we could see the main hero hiking through some mountainous terrain, all pumped up and packing enough fire power to defeat a small army, and the next moment there was this woman telling us about the magical powers of a washing detergent. I eventually figured out what was going on, but the commercial break was soon over and I settled down to watching the rest of the movie. But then ten minutes or so later the same occurred. It was so intrusive and disruptive that it completely turned me off commercial free-to-air television and landed me in Auntie's warm commercial-free embrace.

The ABC! My relationship with the Australian Broadcasting Corporation has been a remarkable journey. It would not be an exaggeration to say that I fell in love with the ABC. Even in these early days I could detect a left-green bias, a tendency to focus on progressive and environmental issues, to report one side of the story more favourably than the other. But that was on a relatively low scale and was tolerable. I generally found most ABC programs to be interesting and informative. I thought ABC presenters were competent and very professional, and that in most cases they were keen to report fully and objectively. I also think most ABC journos made a genuine effort not to allow their own political predilections to influence their reporting.

I loved ABC's news and public affairs programs. Come 7 pm and my TV was invariably tuned to Channel 2 for the evening news. It became a bit of a joke with my daughters – *Don't bother Dad, the ABC news is on*. I adored Richard Morecroft, with his heart-warming smile and the mischievous sparkle in his eyes. The news bulletin was not only very informative, but was often also very entertaining. What I found particularly impressive was that the news team almost invariably managed to find an uplifting side to even the darkest and most distressing story. You rarely went away depressed, pessimistic, upset.

I seldom missed Kerry O'Brian's *7.30 Report*. While he was unable to completely mask his political sympathies, I thought he made a genuine effort to be as tough interviewing his lefty guests as he was with the conservatives.

And I was hungry for more. I started watching Tony Jones on *Lateline*. I admired Jones' immense journalistic skills, his ability to cut through, to pinpoint the most critical issues of the day. I will never forget Jones' interview with Christopher Hitchens. It may have been the last public interview Hitchens gave before he succumbed to his cancer. It was literally heart-breaking. By the time it finished I had tears in my eyes.

There was also *Q&A* and *Insiders*. I found both to be compulsive viewing and almost never missed an episode.

I was probably one of the very first listeners of ABC Newsradio when it started some time in August 1994. I woke up to Russell Powell's deep baritone. Just before the 6.30 news segment he would read out the current temperatures in a number of the world's capital cities, including my native Sofia. (No, we didn't have weather apps then.) I sent him an email to commend the way he pronounced the name of the capital – Sófia, with the stress falling on the first syllable, not Sofia like almost everyone else said it. On the next morning Russell Powell casually mentioned that one of his listeners had complimented him on the way he pronounced the name of the Bulgarian capital. It was hilarious.

I soon became virtually addicted to ABC radio. I purchased a small transistor radio and had it pre-tuned to four stations: AM1458 (ABC Newsradio), AM1512 (Radio National), AM1233 (ABC Newcastle) and FM106.1 (ABC Classic FM). I had my little radio with me wherever I went.

I woke up to Newsradio for my early morning news, then tuned in to RN for their AM program and, following that, RN Breakfast with Peter Thompson. I absolutely loved the guy. He was highly professional, yet kind and even gentle, with a subtle sense of humour. I vividly remember his chats with regular RN contributor Michelle Grattan. The two invariably had a go at the political class and rarely missed a thing. Their exchanges were incisive, but also extremely witty and entertaining. They poked fun at the politicians (no one was spared), but it was never in a sneering, let alone malicious, way. We all – the host, his guest and the listeners – had a laugh and a really good time.

Now switch to the present moment. I still wake up to Newsradio (some habits die really hard), but rarely manage to endure a full news segment. I no longer tune in to RN. It has been a few years since I last watched a *Q&A* or an *Insiders* episode. What happened? Has it been me that changed so much or has it been the ABC? Probably a little bit of both. As people age, they naturally tend to become a little more conservative in their outlook. It would be unreasonable to assume that I have somehow ducked this trend. At the same time the ABC was undergoing a shift in the opposite direction. My sense is that their shift to the left was considerably stronger than my shift to the right.

Obviously this breakup did not occur overnight. It is hard to pinpoint the exact moment when it all started – probably around a dozen years or so ago. It was almost imperceptible when it started, but gradually I became aware of a growing ABC tendency to focus on trendy lefty causes, in particular climate change, refugees and Indigenous affairs. I felt increasingly turned off by the ever growing chorus of voices – both reporters and commentators – almost invariably representing only one side of the public debate. I think Barry Cassidy's *Insiders* was the first ABC show that I abandoned. This was followed in short order by *Lateline* and *Q&A*, then by RN. I remained faithful to the *7 pm News* and to *7.30* a bit longer. (I still have a lot of respect and admiration for *7.30*'s Leigh Sales – one of the most talented journos of her generation, although Leigh too has been unable to completely disguise her political biases. Do you remember her first interview with Malcolm Turnbull after he became PM? I bet she now would rather forget it.) But my loyalty to the ABC was gradually wearing out. The news was no longer about reporting the news, it was quickly becoming an act of political activism. In front of my eyes, the ABC was turning into a propaganda machine.

Out of habit I would continue to tune in to the *7 pm News*, but would mute the sound and only unmute it for the sports segment and the weather. But then I noticed that the sport segment was no longer so much about sporting competitions and achievements, but about identity issues in the field of sport, like alleged racial abuse or domestic violence against women, etc. And I limited my exposure to the weather segment alone. You see, I lived under the illusion that the weather report was one thing which could not be contaminated by lefty propaganda. And then one nice evening Graham Creed was telling us about some unusually cool temperatures around the state, and he hastened to "reassure" his viewers that this abnormally cold spell does not constitute evidence against global warming. Since when did Creed become a climatologist rather than a glorified reader of the day's temperatures? And to top this, one Sunday night in November (17 November 2019, to be precise) Juanita Phillips instructed her viewers to expect a hot 26 degrees in Sydney on the following day. A **hot** 26 (twenty-six) degrees? What kind of insanity was that? It would be very hard to imagine more perfect weather conditions than a balmy sunny 26 degrees.

Thus ended my ABC journey.

It would be unfair not to acknowledge that political activism on the left is not exclusive to the ABC, and more or less of it can be found on commercial TV and in most of the print media. There seems to be a strongly growing trend among many of the media to recognise their principal function as advocates, not as reporters – they are not here to inform us, but to persuade us, even indoctrinate us. Because so many of the journos nowadays are pursuing a political or an ideological goal, we regularly see very selective reporting whereby some issues are reported ad nauseam (like climate change), while others are deliberately ignored. We also increasingly see reporting which is essentially dishonest whereby an issue is deliberately misrepresented in order to fit a preferred narrative. Remember the story we heard on the "news" – about the woman who told ScoMo, *You are not my Prime Minister*; notably the reporters failed to mention a "minor" detail, viz., that the woman was a UK citizen and that her words were a statement of fact, not a political rebuke.

And again, to be fair, the conservative-leaning media (to the extent that there are any left at all) are not immune to bias either. Sky News' Paul Murray is a straight shooter who does not usually hold back, regardless of which side of politics is in his target. But have you heard him say anything critical of Scott Morrison, even once? When have you ever heard Peta Credlin criticise her former boss Tony Abbott?

But while the taxpayer funded national broadcaster's charter mandates ABC journos "to uphold the fundamental journalistic principles of accuracy and impartiality," there are no such impositions on the commercial media. They are a free player – they can do whatever they like. They can choose to be as biased or unbiased as they wish. But they should never forget that as the fourth estate they wield enormous power and should never lose sight of the responsibly which comes with it.

Returning briefly to where I started, given the nature and functions of the media in the communist Bulgaria I grew up in, it was only after I arrived in Australia that I started to truly appreciate the vital role that the media play in a pluralistic society, with one exception. One lesson that the communist regime in Bulgaria did teach me in a very compelling fashion was that propaganda works, and can in fact be extremely effective in influencing people's thinking.

Let us take again a brief detour down Bulgaria's history lane. In the 13th century Bulgaria was one of the first European countries to be run over by the then ascendant Ottoman Empire. Bulgaria effectively remained an Ottoman province for over 500 years, until almost the end of the 19th c. During this period a sizable Turkish minority settled on the territory of contemporary Bulgaria. Most of them lived alongside native Bulgarians in a remarkably harmonious and conflict-free relationship. After the Russian-Turkish War of 1877-78 and the liberation of Bulgaria, many of these ethnic Turkish settlers chose to remain in Bulgaria. After centuries of often really brutal Ottoman rule, it would not have been particularly surprising to see the newly freed Bulgarians take on the Turkish settlers, and seek revenge for five centuries of oppression and injustice. It did not happen. It speaks volumes of the remarkable tolerance, good will and generosity of spirit of Bulgarians that their Turkish neighbours suffered no abuse or recriminations.

This happy state of co-existence between the Bulgarian majority and the ethnic Turkish minority continued for a whole century. Then in the middle of the 1980s the communist Government of Bulgaria undertook a reckless criminal act of biblical proportions, an act of ethnic cleansing. They started forcibly changing the ethnic Turks' names with Bulgarian ones. It was cynically called "the Revival Process." And it was done in a very brutal fashion. Army divisions were dispatched to occupy settlements with mostly Turkish population. In some places cemeteries were vandalised and tombstones wearing ethnic Turkish names were destroyed. People who refused to comply were incarcerated and subjected to physical and psychological torment. Some lost their lives.

This brutal treatment caused a mass exodus. Over 300 000 ethnic Turks packed their most valuable belonging into cars, trucks, even horse carts and, over the course of several months, crossed the border into neighbouring Turkey. They had been forced to abandon their houses, their livelihoods and the country which had been their home for many generations.

And then the regime's formidable propaganda apparatus kicked into action. Television, radio, newspapers, every existing media outlet showed us the caravans moving South towards the Turkish border. The Turks involved in this mass exodus were decent ordinary hard-working people, most commonly farmers or blue-collar workers, mums and dads, children and babies, grandparents. They were mocked by the media, they were ridiculed, they were labelled "tourists" going on an "excursion", they were condemned for "deserting their motherland."

This propaganda campaign was utterly grotesque, yet it was phenomenally successful. It managed to generate a wave of ferocious anti-Turkish sentiment among the ethnic Bulgarians.

And this sentiment was not short-lived by any standard. It easily outlasted the propaganda campaign and even a decade later – long after the "revival" madness had been abandoned – had not completely dissipated. What really stunned and terrified me was how effective and far-reaching the propaganda was. It was able to contaminate the minds of even highly educated and otherwise very sensible people, including people I knew socially and even (dare I admit) some relations. There were clearly thinking people among them, people who had no illusions about the communist regime and who previously had rarely taken seriously anything they had heard or seen on the state-controlled media. And now they chose to believe the absurd "excursionist" narrative of the propaganda machine.

As the reader can surmise, this prompted quite a few fiery arguments and cost me a few friends and acquaintances. But this personal dimension of the story is unimportant. The important part is that it gave me a glimpse at the astonishing power that the media possess, perhaps more so than any other institution. Power to induce sweeping changes in the public consciousness. Power, which when used constructively and professionally, can be of tremendous benefit to the community; but which can cause enormous harm when used capriciously or maliciously. Power which should be used to seek the truth and report it, and to hold political and public leaders to account, rather than for political activism and for moral posturing.

With great power comes great responsibility. This is particularly valid for the Australian Broadcasting Corporation which as the public broadcaster must be held to the highest standard.

Epilogue

Is This the End of the Fairy Tale?

As I detailed in previous chapters, the start of my Australian journey was marked by the typical cultural shock, and my early days here were marred by bouts of nostalgia and financial hardship. In time, the culture shock quite typically passed, the financial problems were gradually alleviated and the nostalgia eventually subsided. Then came a period of growing admiration for my new country – admiration for the extraordinary success and prosperity that the Aussies had managed to accomplish through very hard work (and, admittedly, a little bit of luck).

I remember a conversation with my late mother. It took place during my first visit back to the old country in 1999. She was lamenting Bulgaria's deteriorating living standards and was blaming the West for its failure to provide meaningful assistance to help us out of our economic predicament. She justifiably accused the West of hypocrisy. As my mother pointed out, these were the same guys that for decades had decried the evils of communism and the suffering of the nations under it. They were the ones that wholeheartedly welcomed the collapse of Soviet communism and vocally celebrated the former socialist bloc's transition to democracy. Yet they did not move a finger to help these nations in this difficult transition. All undeniably true.

But then I thought – whoever helped the Aussies build **their** beautiful country? Remember, the early settlers started virtually from scratch in a completely undeveloped territory, in a harsh and often hostile natural environment. They developed the land for agriculture, explored the mineral resources, built the cities and the infrastructure. No one from without came to assist. They did it all by themselves. And for that they fully deserved my admiration.

As the years passed, my admiration started gradually to be replaced by a growing sense of lost opportunity.

I can see so much opportunity here that it literally boggles the mind. In terms of its geographical location, landmass, and mineral and agricultural resources Australia has a practically infinite potential for wealth generation. If properly and judiciously explored, it can make Australia self-sufficient and completely independent of the rest of the world, unimaginably wealthy, the greatest country on earth. It can make every single Australian a billionaire.

The fact that we do not see this happening is heart-breaking. When was the last time that Australia was actually involved in nation building? How long has it been since a new dam was constructed? What about a new railroad? Superfast modern trains travelling at up to 300 km/h have long been a reality in many other countries around the world, including developing countries like China. In today's Australia it still takes a glacial two and a half hours to manage the stupefying distance of 150 km between Newcastle and Sydney – not much faster than a century ago.

Our country's elites have wilfully chosen to leave this potential unexplored. This is not just a disgrace – it is an act of abject betrayal.

The Government's energy policy is another monumental failure.

Epilogue

Modernity is energy intensive. Practically every aspect of life in an advanced economy crucially depends on energy – not only to heat our houses in winter and to stay cool in summer, but also for industry, for transport, agriculture, refrigeration. High living standards are contingent on the availability of abundant, cheap and reliable energy. You would think that, in view of this, ensuring the availability of abundant, cheap and reliable energy will be the Government's highest priority. You would think wrong. Indeed, few other things illustrate more compellingly the West's abandonment of reason than the fashion in which our "leaders" have handled "climate change" and the associated energy policy. Their determination to cancel carbon dioxide – a naturally occurring gas of critical importance to plant growth and to life generally – is just one side of the folly. The other side of the folly relates to **how** they are planning to achieve reductions in carbon dioxide emissions. They intend to do this (have indeed already started doing it) by replacing cheap and reliable coal and gas generators of electricity with expensive and unreliable solar and wind generators. Let's put aside the undeniable fact that few things are more destructive to the natural environment than the solar and wind farms. What completely defies logic and reason is the politicians' adamant refusal to consider nuclear and hydro generation of electricity. Because there is no safer and more environmentally friendly form of energy than nuclear, with hydro coming a very close second. Building a dam may inconvenience a couple of frogs and a few snails. So what? The payoff is enormous – you get to store one of the most precious finite resources (water) and you get abundant 100% clean cheap reliable electricity.

The politicians' reckless abandonment of reliable sources of energy and the relentless push towards more and more intermittent renewables can only have one outcome – a situation when Australians will no longer be able to press the switch and confidently expect the lights to come on. This moment will come much sooner than most people expect, indeed has already started happening here and there.

About a year ago, it did happen to me on a very hot summer's night. After an extremely hot day, in order to get a reasonable night's sleep, I decided to leave the aircon on during the night. I do it very infrequently, never more than half a dozen times in a year. I woke up around 1 am covered in sweat. Power was off. The temperature was still in the low 30s. It was extremely uncomfortable.

This lasted several hours.

Obviously I had no way of knowing what caused the outage, although I suspect that the system simply couldn't cope with the demand. At this time of the 24 hour cycle most people were at home and most would have had the aircon running. It was dark and there wasn't a whiff of breeze in the air, therefore not a single watt of electricity was coming from solar and wind sources.

So what, someone might say? It was no more than a passing inconvenience, stop whingeing. In my recollection of the event it wasn't a mere inconvenience – it was extremely uncomfortable, verging on physical suffering. Indeed, remaining for hours in these conditions could be life-threatening for people with serious health problems, for the older and the frail. But even if we only saw it as an inconvenience, why should we have to endure such inconveniences in a first-world country in the 21st century? It is completely unnecessary, it is self-inflicted, we have become slaves to a mindless ideology.

We know that power outages have also occurred elsewhere, in particular Victoria and South Australia.

Epilogue

Until quite recently, I had always thought that electricity shortages and blackouts were a trade mark of the communist/socialist world. What greater indictment can there be of Australia's ruling class than their failure to ensure affordable and reliable electricity for the country? It shows lack of leadership, political impotence, cowardice, an act of betrayal. And it will be the weakest and the most vulnerable members of the community who will suffer the consequences of this betrayal. They will freeze in winter and boil in summer, because they cannot afford the electricity bill. The Malcolm Turnbulls of this world will not feel a pinch if their electricity bill was 20 times higher – they would not give it a second thought.

In the weeks and months leading up to the 2019 "unwinnable" election when almost everyone predicted an easy Labor win, I was getting increasingly anxious. I felt particularly uneasy about Labor's reckless renewable energy targets and the unavoidable energy shortages that would come as a consequence. I was so worried that I started thinking of purchasing a small diesel generator, so that I can avoid becoming hostage to Labor's energy folly. ScoMo's "miracle" election win spared me a few thousand dollars. Or so I thought at the time. Meanwhile, however, the PM has changed his tune on climate change and it looks increasingly likely that the acquisition of a diesel generator has only been delayed by a few years.

In the introductory chapter of this book I briefly spoke about issues of identity (including identity conflict) that are almost invariably associated with immigration. Erosion and loss of original identity can be a very disagreeable experience which some immigrants struggle to cope with. It is not uncommon at all for long-term immigrants to return, upon retirement, to the old country and spend the autumn of their lives there.

Personally, I have always been very comfortable with my mixed Bulgarian-Australian identity. While I was always happy to visit the old country, I never had even a remote desire to go back on a permanent basis. Australia was my home.

I remember a conversation I had a few years ago with my ethnic brother and (conservative) soulmate Ivan, also an Australian resident of more than 20 years. Ivan was then a senior research fellow at CSIRO and was struggling with what he perceived as the lax work ethic and even incompetence at this government funded institution. He confessed that he was seriously thinking of retiring and going back to Bulgaria. *Don't be an idiot!* I told him. *You have been away for so many years. You have forgotten what life in Bulgaria is like. The reality there will drive you crazy.*

I am not sure how much impression my statement then made on Ivan, in all probability very little. The following year he and his wife Silvia took an extended holiday in Bulgaria. Shortly after they came back, Ivan told me – *We are not going back*!

Quite recently I was chatting with my sister Marta (in Bulgaria) on Zoom and she was telling me about a friend of hers who, after two decades of residence in Germany, had returned permanently to Bulgaria. *What about you, brother?* Marta asked. *When are you returning?*

In the wake of this conversation I caught myself thinking that the idea of going back, permanently, is not as inconceivable as it had seemed until very recently. This was a rather startling realisation which prompted a fair deal of self-reflection, as well as an attempt to pinpoint the reasons which have caused this (massive) change of heart. I came to the conclusion that it was not a case of suddenly developing an irresistible nostalgia for the old country. It was a case of becoming increasingly dissatisfied with the state

Epilogue

of affairs in the new country. It occurred to me that, very much as with my failed love affair with the ABC, Australia has turned into a direction moving away from me.

As I described in Chapter 1, immense admiration of the liberal democracies of the West was a big part of my adolescence in communist Bulgaria. I admired the West for its prosperity, science and innovation, artistic creativity. Above all I admired the West for its democracy and its freedom. Alas, the contemporary West is by far not what it used to be 50 or 30 or even ten years ago.

Many of my concerns with what has been happening with the West I have voiced elsewhere in this book, but what I find particularly troubling is the erosion of personal freedom. The much celebrated freedom of Western democracy has in recent years dwindled to something which is barely observable with the naked eye. This is a trend which will have profound consequences for Western societies generally.

As Konstantin Kisin (of *Triggernometry* fame) rightly points out, democracy, freedom, prosperity – these are not a given. Westerners do not enjoy them solely as a birth right. Democracy, freedom, prosperity are in fact very frail and it does not take much to undermine them, to have them eroded, to lose them. Kisin was born and raised in the former Soviet Union, later emigrated to the UK. He knows. He says: "If you start messing with the basic formula [of freedoms and democratic rights], these things will go. If you start shutting down freedom of speech, that doesn't only have an impact on freedom of speech, it has an impact on democracy and [a diminished] democracy has an impact on prosperity … and you will end up in a place a lot worse than you have."

This erosion of personal freedom has already been going on in the West for a while. As people get more prosperous and more comfortable, they tend to attach less importance to freedom and start valuing other things (safety, in particular) more.

More recently a new "player" has strongly emerged on the scene. Something akin to a cultural revolution carried by the intellectual, political and media elites has further diminished individual freedom, indeed has had an alarmingly suffocating effect on freedom of speech and on the free exchange of ideas.

As history has unequivocally shown, revolutions are bad. They cause death and destruction and are invariably followed by decades of poverty and misery.

The political and cultural elites forcibly impose upon the rest of us their own morality, their own values. It is an increasingly intolerant new thinking – a form of new totalitarianism, a brutal cancel culture severely punishing anyone who dares to voice a view which even remotely departs from the new progressive ideology.

To make things worse, this new morality is almost entirely detached from reality. These new values are incompatible with well-established facts and truths. Much of the West's unparalleled success can be attributed to its insatiable quest for knowledge. That is now over. A mindless new religion has chosen to abandon, indeed to unlearn, the immense body of knowledge derived over centuries of scientific exploration and rational thought.

In *The Weekend Australian* (14 December 2019), Chris Kenny laments what he perceives as the demise of Aussie stoicism. "Rational arguments, hard facts and intelligent debate have been cast aside in favour of woke whingeing", Kenny says. This extraordinary disregard for established facts, for sound empirical

Epilogue

evidence, diminishes the nation's ability to pursue solid rational policies and to find effective ways of tackling the nation's problems. Failure to return to reasoned debate based on facts and evidence can lead to the nation's demise. As Mark Steyn once said, societies can become too stupid to survive.

All this strikes a terrifying resemblance to the world of communist Bulgaria in which I spent the first half of my life, where people were not only required to accept the absurd dogmas of an inhumane ideology, but were also expected to repeat them with conviction, to chant them with sincere enthusiasm – like a primitive tribe mouthing the mystical words and expressions that the high priest feeds them.

Do you remember the hit comedy show *Two and a Half Men*? When the main character is due to take part in couples counselling, his brother Alan instructs him: "You have to be able to fake sincerity, Charlie!" Back in the old days we had become masters of faking sincerity. We were unmistakably sincere when we proclaimed our profound gratitude to the Bulgarian Communist Party for their stellar leadership, for our Leaders' selfless care of the citizenry, for the immense good that they had brought to our lives. We were unmistakably sincere when we celebrated the astounding achievements of socialism. We spoke with unmistakable conviction when we asserted that our living standards were immensely superior to those in the West and that we were the happiest human beings on the face of the planet. But, of course, it was not a comedy show. Failure to fake sincerity was mercilessly punished, including forced labour and imprisonment.

Obviously the new cultural totalitarianism of the West has not (yet) gone so far. People do not (yet) get jailed for expressing "unapproved" views. But they do get punished in ways which can utterly destroy their lives. They get "cancelled", they get publicly ostracised, they lose their jobs and their livelihood.

Day in, day out, I witness examples of this mindlessness, this abandonment of reason and common sense, this relentless assertion of fake facts, fake news, fake norms and values. And alongside it comes this relentless pressure on all of us not only to accept them, but to wholeheartedly embrace them – with all of the fake sincerity we can muster.

Well, to use another famous film reference, I am too old for this shit.

This more than anything else can compel me to pack my bags and take the return trip to the old country. If it does come to that, I will do it with an open mind. I have no illusions that going back will be easy. It will involve a culture shock as severe as the one I experienced on arrival here. It will require serious readjustments and compromises, acceptance of social and cultural values that I have long stopped identifying with. But if I am spared the humiliation of having to fake sincerity, it will be a price worth paying. Because one thing is certain. My fellow Bulgarians – for all of their flaws and imperfections – have not lost their minds, have not abandoned reason and common sense.

And here we finally come to the question quizzically posed in the title of this book – Is the Australian fairy tale coming to an end?

A dispassionate examination of the country's state of affairs will show a picture which is not particularly confidence inspiring. We see mountains of public and private indebtedness, very little or no political leadership, no clear vision for the future of this country, let alone the will and determination to pursue it. Instead, we see the country's elites embrace a mindless and very destructive new ideology representing a new model of totalitarianism. We see

Epilogue

the inexorable attrition of individual freedom. The "liberal" in "liberal democracy" is just about to disappear. One wonders what will happen to the "democracy" part once the "liberal" is gone.

One does not need to be a total pessimist to recognise that the country's current trajectory does not look good.

Is this trajectory irreversible? Has Australia's situation become irredeemable? With all my heart I wish the answer to these questions is "No", but I honestly do not know.

In deliberating Australia's current plight, we should not ignore the fact that these processes are not exclusively Australian, that Australia is a part of a much broader trend encompassing most of Europe and North America. The good news is that there are aspects of Australia's situation which can be seen as comparatively advantageous. For one, the inroads that the new cultural revolution has made here are not as deep as they are elsewhere, particularly in the USA and the UK. Perhaps more importantly, Australia does not have a history of slavery, nor the appalling legacy of racial division they have in America and to a lesser degree also in the UK. The societal divisions here are by far not as profound as they are in America.

If this is all true, it means that the task of reversing the current trajectory will not be as hard as elsewhere. By no means easy, but hopefully not impossible.

So what is to be done? The only way forward that I can see is for the "Quiet Australians" to stop being quiet and to become vocal. Let us not forget that the people carrying the new cultural revolution are a tiny minority. Yes, an extremely powerful and vocal minority, but a minority nonetheless. If we, the Quiet Australians, chose to raise our voices even a little, we will drown the new high priests' hysterical screams.

So – speak up and speak out, it is as simple and as easy as that. But is it really? If my personal experience is anything to go by, speaking out is neither simple, nor easy. If it had been, I would have done it years ago. I didn't. I chose to remain silent all these years. Having seen the brutal cancel culture in action can have a rather chilling effect on one's desire to go against the new orthodoxy. It is not an admirable thing to admit, but the truth is I was too scared to speak out. For decades I had worked extremely hard to make something of my life, personally and professionally. The possibility of having my life's achievement (for what it's worth) taken away from me was truly terrifying.

No, choosing to become vocal and to stand up to the new totalitarians is not easy by any stretch of the imagination. I also think most ordinary Aussies are too busy managing their lives, too preoccupied with the daily chores and cares to pay too much attention to the chants of the new high priests. They should start paying attention though, because in a not too distant future they will lose their ability to lead their lives in the way they choose, their control over their lives will be taken away. They will be required to pledge their fealty to the new totalitarians or will not be allowed to run a business, buy a house, go to university, travel overseas.

Writing this book has been my way of raising my voice. I wish I had done it earlier, but hopefully it is not too late. This book is my way of calling on my fellow Quiet Australians. Unless you are prepared to lose the miracle that Australia has become, you too raise your voice and make sure it is heard loud and clear.

Newcastle, November 2021

www.ingramcontent.com/pod-product-compliance
Lightning Source LLC
Chambersburg PA
CBHW070359240426
43671CB00013BA/2561